Like Water on Leaves of Taro

A Himalayan Memoir

Tulasi Acharya

Colorful Crow Publishing

Like Water on Leaves of Taro: A Himalayan Memoir

Copyright © 2025 by Tulasi Acharya

Cover Copyright © 2025 by Amber Lanier Nagle

All rights reserved. No portion of this book may be reproduced, stored in a retrieval system, or transmitted in any form or by any means—electronic, mechanical, photocopying, recording, or otherwise—without the prior written permission of the publisher, except as permitted by U.S. copyright law.

Published by Colorful Crow Publishing

Calhoun, GA

www.colorfulcrowpublishing.com

ISBN 978-1-964271-28-6 (hardcover)

ISBN 978-1-964271-30-9 (eBook)

ISBN 978-1-964271-29-3 (paperback)

Printed in the United States of America

First Edition, October 2025

10 9 8 7 6 5 4 3 2 1

For all who have stood in the shadow of loss,
whose tears have fallen into the holy river,
and who still carry the names—and the light—of their beloved forward.

Advance Praise for *Like Water on Leaves of Taro*

"In *Like Water on Leaves of Taro*, Tulasi Acharya approaches personal loss with both emotional honesty and intellectual depth. Weaving his family's private sorrow with the global tragedy of theCOVID-19 pandemic, Acharya explores the limits of human endurance through a kaleidoscope of cultural, generational, and spiritual perspectives.

His prose is mesmerizing—soft, lyrical, and deeply affecting. Acharya beautifully portrays the love and respect that binds his family, tenderly illustrating their struggle to make sense of a dark and complex world. With arresting clarity, he plunges readers into the vivid landscape of grief and the universal need to find meaning in loss. Ultimately, this memoir offers a stirring testament to the healing power of reflection, memory, and hope."
—**The Book Life Prize**

"Acharya takes us on a heartfelt journey into life's fragility and grief, but at every turn he reminds us that love and hope give light in dark places. Nepal may offer a foreign setting to many readers, but the emotional territory of this memoir is familiar and will reward."
—**Anthony Grooms**, Georgia Writers Hall of Fame inductee and award-winning author of *Bombingham* and *The Vain Conversation*

"Tulasi Acharya's *Like Water on Leaves of Taro: A Himalayan Memoir* invites readers into the psychological interiority of his grief, fears, and struggles as he faces serious illness, death, and endless sadness of his beloved family members—all set in international and pandemic cultural contexts. Honest, straightforward, and provocative—this emotional memoir from a father's, husband's, son's, son-in-law's, college professor's perspectives—is an important contribution to the memoir genre."
—**Beverly J. Armento**, Award-winning author, *Seeing Eye Girl: A Memoir of Madness, Resilience, and Hope*"

"*Like Water on Leaves of Taro*, Tulasi Acharya's poignant memoir invites readers into a deeply personal story shaped by love, loss, and the shifting ground beneath a family caught between continents and generations. With lyrical honesty, Tulasi reflects on fatherhood, grief, and the rituals that hold us together—even as the world around us unravels. Set against the rich landscape of Nepal and shadowed by a global pandemic, this is a moving meditation on resilience, responsibility, and the fragile beauty of everyday life."
—**Robert Gwaltney**, award-winning author of *The Cicada Tree*

"In *Like Water on Leaves of Taro*, while Acharya's homecoming is filled with frustration and grief, readers, especially those mourning the loss of a relative or friend, will appreciate and find comfort in his quiet reflection on what gives his life real substance and meaning—good health, being present to the moment, and cherishing and remembering those he loves."
—**Kristine F. Anderson**, author of the award-winning *Crooked Truth* and the award-winning *Crooked Lines*

"Acharya's marvelous memoir uncovers with deft words the slicing and severing of life that death brings both in quickness and slow motion. The writer watches death, and in its misery, he also sees seeds of hope—life pushing through like blades of grass in cracked concrete—pulling his family back from the brink of an abyss of despair In Acharya's heartfelt ode to death, he reminds us that the dead live on—that in quiet moments they return, and with them comes a joy gently tinged with sorrow."
—**Dr. Kay Traille**, Professor of History Education at Kennesaw State University

"*Like Water on Leaves of Taro: A Himalayan Memoir* presents events and context from a fresh and honest perspective. The book highlights societal reluctance to openly discuss illnesses like cancer, especially with children, and this dynamic is artfully portrayed in the book. The writer has vividly and honestly portrayed the family calamity in the book."
—**Prakash Sayami**, Nepali Film Director, writer, and producer

"*Like Water on Leaves of Taro: A Himalayan Memoir* is an interdisciplinary text, which not only reflects the agonizing situation of the writer's spouse but also contributes to building public awareness about cancer. The book is a health awareness toolkit, while simultaneously conveying a family tragedy."
—**Gita Tripathee**, Nepali poet, lyricist, essayist, literary critic, and scholar

"The author's mastery of mystery and suspense is vividly apparent by how the reader is gripped through the final page of the book."
—**Gopi Krishna Dhungana**, Sub-editor of *Annapurna Post*

"The writer is engrossed in life, death, and meaningful life, with extensive references from philosophers, poets, essayists, and ethicists. The allusions range from a revered Hindu scripture, 'Mahabharat', and from 'Waste Land', a seminal modern poem by TS Eliot. The invocation of philosophy on the termination of life and yearning to seek meaning makes the book meditative and literary."
—**Narayan Ghimire**, Editor, *New Agency of Nepal RSS*

"This raw and riveting memoir offers a unique perspective on the author's experience of loss and love, death and birth within his family. Acharya pursues a Kafkaesque quest to navigate the tattered infrastructure of a health care system while honoring timeless rituals and social expectations as he seeks aid for his ailing father-in-law and grieving wife. By turns heart-stopping and poignant, this beautifully written work gives us a glimpse into the complex and intimate process of death and shows us ways to heal our souls after losses great and small. A must-read memoir!"
—**Bridget Pupillo**, Editor

"*Like Water on Leaves of Taro* is more than a pandemic memoir—it is a universal story of loss, resilience, and love. With exquisite sensitivity, Dr. Tulasi Acharya explores the immigrant's dilemma of distance and duty, the sacred bonds of family, and the redemptive power of hope even in the face of devastating grief. Set against the beauty and complexity of Nepal, his words evoke the intimacy of caregiving, the weight of tradition, and the humanity found in our shared rituals of mourning and survival."
—**Candice Louisa Daquin**, Managing Editor, Lit Fox Books

"This memoir by Dr. Acharya, focuses on various dimensions and experiences of life and death. Death is inevitable. This book also confirms that death cannot be avoided."
—**Padam Bhattarai** in *Annapurna Post*

"The strength of this book lies in its simple presentation and reflection about life and death. In times of trouble, we often experience ambiguity and wonder what now? What next? In his book, *Like Water on Leaves of Taro: A Himalayan Memoir*, author Dr. Tulasi Acharya openly talks about life and death by candidly approaching the subject in a clear and simple manner designed to resonate with us all."
—**Badri Prasad Dhakal**, Author

"*Like Water on Leaves of Taro* is an incredibly heartbreaking memoir that tells of the shared experiences of a family coming to terms with an unimaginable and untimely loss. This memoir is a poignant read."
—**Elizabeth Howard**, Assistant Branch Manager Calhoun-Gordon County Library

Contents

1. Like Water on Leaves of Taro — 1
2. Memories — 18
3. Branch of an Uprooted Tree — 24
4. Humans, Rivers, and the Tears of Mountains — 30
5. Smoke and Smile's Longevity — 37
6. American Dream's Flight — 47
7. Truth's Pain and Illusion's Joy — 54
8. Another Witness to the End — 60
9. Ph.D. Title and the Rising Darkness — 63
10. The Riddle of Palliative Care — 67
11. Pollution, Pranayama, and Profession — 71
12. Power of Poetry — 73
13. Hollow Body on a Faded Couch — 76
14. Celebration of Death — 80
15. Difficulty of Hiding the Truth — 84
16. Declaration of God's Death — 88
17. Sightseers — 92
18. When Mountain Becomes Flute — 97

19.	Prisoner of Indecisiveness on Depression Day	100
20.	Whistle of a Riddled Heart	105
21.	Email, Dipang Lake, and Cards	107
22.	The Light of a Lamp About to Die	113
23.	Fate of Hamlet	117
24.	News	121
25.	Fear of Saturday	123
26.	Attachment	125
27.	Dhido, Weed, and Manisha	129
28.	Discussion of Patient's Rights	133
29.	After Shedding Loads from the Heart	137
30.	Morphine Invites Death	142
31.	Fear of COVID-19 and Hope for a Miracle	148
32.	Fear, Horror, and a Day of Disturbance	153
33.	Pass, Breath, and Hope in Lockdown	156
34.	Dreams Rest in Seti River	164
35.	Unfulfilled Dreams	169
36.	Reflection on Death	171
37.	Imageries	173
38.	Rites	176
39.	Death: Lessons	181

Chapter One

Like Water on Leaves of Taro

November 30, 2019

Because of jetlag, I woke at five o'clock, an hour early. It was six o'clock when my daughter Krisha woke up and started suckling at her mother's breasts. Looking into Krisha's eyes enveloped me in a sense of warmth, akin to a river's gentle cascade, drenching me with love and a connection to my child. A surge of responsibility and awe erupted within me, marking my first experience as a father. This profound feeling, impossible to capture in words, filled me with purpose and joy, making my life meaningful as I embraced the role of caring for my child.

"When are you planning to visit Nepal?" Kripa asked.

The past two months in America had been punctuated by my wife Kripa's persistent request—a plea I now vividly recalled.

"Please return home to celebrate Krisha's upcoming birthday," she said "and your own achievements as well. I am excited about that."

Arrival in Nepal came just the day before, coinciding with the Christmas holiday. Four months had passed since completing my Ph.D. and beginning my role as an assistant professor of English in the U.S.

This trip wasn't about me.

I was going home for my daughter's first birthday—a milestone I couldn't miss. She was only two weeks old when I left. Now, I ached to make up for lost time: to hold her, hear her laugh, and somehow show her how proud I was to be her father.

There was also the hope of sitting beside my family, letting them hold a copy of my newly published book, watching their faces light up as I spoke of my teaching position in America.

From across the ocean, they had cheered me on.

Now, I longed to share it all in person.

In the back of my mind, I was already making plans to bring them to the U.S. and build something brighter together, even if I wasn't yet sure what the future held for me.

In the morning, Kripa loved to sleep in a bit. Her eyes remained closed, like *lajjawati jhar*—the shame-laden shrub. She lay quietly on the bed, breastfeeding. With careful steps, I made my way to the bathroom, not wanting to disturb the stillness. Kathmandu held a deeper chill than I remembered from my last visit.

A twist of the tap sent water gushing out—cold as frost-covered iron. Hands cupped beneath the stream, I splashed a few drops onto my face, murmuring *achhuchhuchu* through the sting.

At the sound of my voice, Krisha paused mid-nurse, lifting her head from her mother's breast.

"Can you please take her with you to play? I would like to sleep a bit more," Kripa said, halfway between awakening and unconsciousness, her eyes still shut.

With gentle hands, the baby was lifted and placed carefully onto the red carpet. A clean diaper, warm clothes—each step done with care. Her small limbs offered slight resistance; this man was still unfamiliar to her. Not yet the father she recognized, only the voice she had heard through a screen.

From America, my voice reached her often—video calls at odd hours, stories spun across the screen that she couldn't yet understand, save for a few sacred words: *baba, mama.*

Each time, the ache to reach through and hold her had to be swallowed.

Now, even with her so near, closeness would take time. In the ways that matter most—touch, scent, presence—I remained a stranger.

Meanwhile, I worked through the long list of paperwork to bring my family to the U.S.—to close the distance once and for all.

To cheer up my daughter, I began singing a Nepali song by Prakash Shrestha: "*Timro aankhako sagarama lahar lahar daudirahechh—in the ocean of your eyes, the waves rippled.*" I gazed into her eyes and said, "Your grandmother—your mother's mother—is coming from Pokhara to see you today."

She formed her lips into an O shape, giving me the impression she understood what I said. Because of my father-in-law's chronic illness, he and my mother-in-law were coming to Kathmandu that morning for his treatment, and we waited for their arrival.

Memories of last night's video call with my mother-in-law flooded back. "Okay, Mummy, we'll see you tomorrow and talk," I said.

Her smile warmed my heart through the screen. I recalled her excitement about our visit after a year apart. My wife's mother found an excellent doctor for her husband in the capital city of Nepal.

"Within an hour's time my father could manage to butcher a live goat and get the meat ready for cooking," Kripa used to say with pride. "My father was our source of inspiration, our strong faith in the family."

He had recently lost twenty-five kilograms in two months and continued to lose weight. His health deteriorated by the day. Along with the weight, his appetite had faded. He was often dizzy and exhausted. For the past two years, he had been managing diabetes and taking insulin twice a day.

"He appeared strong at the end of last year's *Dashain* when he put *tika* on our foreheads and gave us his blessing, but when I saw him recently, he no longer resembled himself. To think how much he changed in such a short time!" Kripa said the night before, her eyes welling up. "I want to see him hale and hearty again like he was before."

The immense pain her father's illness inflicted on her became suddenly, painfully clear.

A silent wish took shape—for his swift recovery. Once they arrived in Kathmandu, the hope was to take them to the finest hospital, to search out the best treatment possible.

The prospect of bringing joy to Kripa outweighed any happiness for myself or anyone else. In silence, I acknowledged and empathized with the pain she carried. Her joy was my ultimate source of happiness.

"He's only ever been sick once before—when he had an ulcer in his stomach twenty years ago," Kripa told me. "He was around forty-two years old. They practically cut him in two during the surgery to remove it."

"Hey, *Jwaisaap*," my *sasuraba* (father-in-law) exclaimed as he lifted his T-shirt to reveal his gray hair, ribbed chest, and sagging belly. The scar was frightening—large and clearly visible. His body resembled a jute sack, crudely stitched from top to bottom with thick thread and a heavy needle.

"Ouch!" I replied.

I couldn't bear to see it any longer; instinctively, I covered my eyes with my hands. It was as if my own body had been sliced open and hastily stitched back together. The thought of what I'd seen triggered a migraine that lingered for days, a sharp reminder of life's fragility and the relentless shadow of illness looming over us.

"I think I was around twelve years old during the surgery," Kripa had told me. "The doctor said my father would not survive, but a miracle happened. You cannot imagine how much blood and pus my mother and

I had to clean and throw away. My mother's devotion to my father was beyond measure. Words cannot explain."

Listening to her, I had winced in pain and offered a quiet prayer of gratitude to God for the blessings my *sasuraba* had received.

"He bounced back," she told me. "He ate whatever could be easily digested, and his immune system got stronger. He started gaining muscle and weight and before long he was plump and healthy. He ate everything—sour, bitter, spicy, wine, swine—you name it. Nothing gave him trouble."

But twenty years later, he became lethargic, lost weight, and suffered with a searing pain in his stomach. The CT scans and other reports from the labs in Pokhara didn't show anything clearly, so the doctors in Pokhara suggested he go see a specialist in Kathmandu.

My wife always spoke highly of her mother, describing her as a hard-working person who was consistently healthy. She had never needed to take a pain reliever. Her mother managed all the chores in the house without complaint, and never mentioned headaches or any discomfort. She remembered how her mother never shouted at them; they never heard her speak in a raised voice. She was gentle and kind, a source of unwavering strength. Kripa often hoped her words wouldn't tempt fate, but until that moment, her mother had never been sick—not once.

I was always glad for her and her mother, especially in the shadow of her father's illness.

"Guess what?" Kripa exclaimed with a smile. "My mother had turned fifty-three. She was the same age as the renowned Nepali film superstar, *Mahanayak* Rajesh Hamal."

Yet, my *sasuma* appeared older than her actual years—older than Rajesh Hamal himself. The toll of arduous labor was evident in the lines etched across her face, the missing tooth, and the strands of gray in her hair. Despite these visible signs, she radiated a vibrant smile, which defied all her hardships.

"She's the one who raised us—fed us, dressed us, did our hair, kept us clean, and sent us to school," Kripa had explained to me the night before. "When my father was away from home for work, my mom cared for us and managed the household. If she hadn't been around us all the time, we would not be who we are now. We are grown up, married, and have our own families. My parents are happy to find a son-in-law like you who is kind and understanding. They recently stopped running a restaurant and the money they make by renting out the first two floors of the house is enough for them to live and manage. We are also happy to know that the days of my parents' hardships are over, but the only thing that keeps me worried is my father's disease. I wonder whether he will recover or not."

When she said we, she meant herself and her sister Suman.

Her words drew my full attention. Fingers moved gently through her hair—a quiet gesture of comfort—while her trust stirred a deep humility within me.

With conviction, the reassurance came: "Your father will be fine. God is merciful and gracious."

The hope was simple—that she could turn her heart toward the upcoming celebration of our daughter Krisha's birthday.

"Hey, *Kanchhi*, get up," I said. "Aren't your parents coming to see us today? We should clean the house, buy some fresh vegetables and cook a meal. Call them to see if they're already on the bus. Get up."

Kripa stirred only slightly when nudged, pulling the covers tighter and shifting in her sleep.

To soothe Krisha, a soft melody rose in the quiet—a father's lullaby from the Nepali movie *Swarga* (Heaven), where a beloved actor dances with his daughter, singing words that gently plead for her closeness and ask how deeply she loves her father.

The ringing of Kripa's phone broke the flow of my song.

"Kripa, please get it," I said.

Lifting Krisha up, I held her gaze. "We should celebrate your birthday next week, okay?"

A smile spread across my daughter's face, as if she understood every word.

Her angelic expression seemed to fill the room with light.

A moment so pure—it deserved to be held forever.

"Can you answer that for me, please?" Kripa asked in a sleepy voice, her eyes still closed. She was still half asleep.

"It's best if I don't. It's your call, so you should take it," I said.

Kissing sounds floated toward Krisha, and in return came another round of radiant smiles.

"Who is calling? Can you check for me?" she asked, turning over in bed.

I stretched my neck and read the name on the screen. "Not sure. It says Laxman *dai*,"

No sooner did I read the name than she got up and reached for it.

"Why is he calling so early?"

Kripa immediately answered. As soon as Krisha saw her mother sitting up and speaking, she reached for her, wanting to climb into her lap. I gently pulled her close and tapped the camera on my phone, hoping a quick distraction might ease her worry.

Kripa's posture changed, her arm fell limp, and the phone slipped from her hand to the floor. She erupted into loud, uncontrollable sobs. The room echoed with the intensity of her cries as tears streamed down her cheeks, drenching her face. Overwhelmed by emotion, she crumpled onto the bed and buried her face in the pillows.

"What is going on?" I asked. "Oh shit, what the hell happened?"

Fear clutched at my chest at the sight of her tears.

With Krisha in my arms, soothing gestures reached toward Kripa in an effort to calm her.

"Please find out what is wrong with my mother," she said through her sobbing. "I couldn't live if she were harmed. She is in the hospital."

She tried to rise from the bed by grabbing the mattress. She shouted and cried as if she'd lost her mind.

"Laxman *dai* wouldn't call me unless it was something serious."

"Don't be scared," I said, and rubbed her back. "She's in the hospital; doctors are helping her. Try to be calm."

The phone was quickly taken and the number dialed back, all while Krisha rested against my chest. Tears began to well in her eyes as she watched her mother.

"Hello, I am Kripa's husband," I said. "She started crying as soon as she spoke to you. What happened to her mother?"

"*Jwaisaap*, brother-in-law, *Namaste*. I am Kripa's cousin Laxman. I didn't want to tell her everything, but her mother's case is serious. You should bring her here as soon as possible. We will tell you the rest after you get here," Laxman *dai* said and hung up the phone.

My hands and feet trembled. A wave of dizziness hit me, but I forced myself to stay upright—for my wife, for my daughter.

Something was wrong—a weight pressed hard in my chest.

Sasuma. She was supposed to be on her way to Kathmandu with *Sasuraba*. *An accident?* The mind couldn't stitch it together fast enough.

Kripa's sobs mingled with Krisha's cries, swirling around me like static.

My arms reached out, desperate to hold them both, to hush the noise—but the effort fell short.

Grief pulsed through the house.

Eventually, the sound reached my parents' room and pulled them from sleep.

"What happened? What happened?" they asked.

They hurried from their bedroom; eyes filled with terror and puffy with sleep due to the early hour.

"Her mother is in the hospital in Pokhara," I said in a quivering voice. "Laxman *dai*, her cousin, called and said we should go there," I said.

A palm pressed against my forehead, an instinctive attempt to mask the strain etched across my face.

"Don't cry. Don't fret if she is in the hospital," my mother said.

She rubbed Kripa's back and tried to wipe away her tears.

"Please, take me to my mother, *Budho*," my wife pleaded. "Please take me there right now."

In her gaze and grip, I felt it—I was her anchor.

We hurriedly layered clothes over our pajamas.

Shoes went on without socks, and Krisha's scattered clothes—some on the bed, others on the floor—were swept into a bag.

While Kripa pulled on trousers and a T-shirt, her jacket was added hastily, in case the night grew colder.

Two bags came together in a rush and were slung over a shoulder, breath coming fast and shallow.

With Krisha in one arm and Kripa's hand in the other, we stepped into the night. It took only a few minutes to get ready, but by the time we left the house, both were sobbing.

Our house was in Tikathali, Lalitpur.

There was no time to wait for a bus, so a quick scan of the street became a desperate search for a taxi.

Navigating Kripa's grief felt like wandering in a fog, with no space yet to process what was happening or make sense of my own emotions.

Some moments unraveled in such a bewildering rush that thought itself vanished, leaving nothing but an aching emptiness. It was as if my mind had quietly stepped away—no words, no direction, no presence at all.

That mental void swallowed me whole.

Just then, a taxi appeared, circling back after dropping off a passenger. My arm shot up without thinking, flagging it down.

The driver slowed, his eyes scanning our tear-streaked faces, the way we struggled to catch our breath. He gave a small nod.

He would take us to the airport—a mile and a half away.

"Please, Kripa, you must stop crying. We will be there soon. The plane will take half an hour to get there. Remember, your mother is in the hospital, and we will be there in no time. Please wipe your tears," I said.

A gentle rhythm of pats and strokes moved across her back and head, each touch an attempt to steady us both.

Courage had to rise, even as the heart whispered that her mother's condition was grave.

A silent vow took shape—we would reach the hospital in time to see her.

Every thought remained fixed on Kripa and Krisha, their well-being held above all else.

Though Krisha had quieted, her mother still trembled, and the effort to soothe her continued.

Within a few minutes, we arrived at the Kathmandu airport. It was eight in the morning.

No advance booking had been made—there had been no reason to, not until the news of *Sasuma's* condition reached us.

Instead of having Kripa's parents come to us, the journey had shifted in the other direction—to Pokhara.

The bags were handed to Kripa with a quick request to keep them close, and with Krisha in my arms, I began the walk toward the ticket counter.

At the desk, a plea was made: "Sir, can I get two seats for an emergency flight to Pokhara?"

The domestic terminal buzzed with chaos.

Passengers swarmed the space, pushing and shoving, carts rattling under the weight of bags and boxes. Some entered through the carousel area while others spilled out, weaving in and out like threads in a frayed fabric.

Above it all, the sound of planes taking off and landing filled the air.

"*Dai*, there is no ticket for now. We can probably find some for the afternoon."

The representative for Yeti Airlines had a mustache and stern manner. He wasn't paying much attention to me and focused on the computer screen. He clicked the computer mouse repeatedly.

"You can go ask at the Buddha Airlines counter. You may perhaps find something there."

The heat beneath our layered clothes became impossible to ignore—pajamas still clung to our bodies under outer garments, damp with sweat.

A glance at Kripa revealed her silent sobs, shoulders trembling, her cheeks flushed as though all the blood in her body had surged to her face.

"Jesus, please help us," the whisper escaped into the crowded terminal.

The name felt familiar now, shaped by the past ten years, though my roots belonged to a Hindu family.

To me, God had always been larger than names—Jesus, Mohammed, Vishnu—all pointing toward the same divine mercy.

In that moment, Kripa's mother was placed gently into prayer, offered to whatever form that mercy might take.

"Everything will be alright after we get there," I told Kripa.

I pushed a strand of hair behind her ear and tried to wipe her tears before heading to the ticket counter for Buddha Airlines.

"Not now, *dai*," the official at the counter said, as he peered up at me. "We expect some spots at noon."

Kripa crumpled.

"Please bring me to my mother right now," she sobbed. "Please bring me to my mother right now. Otherwise, I will die here."

She dropped to her knees, not being able to stand on her feet. It felt a bit dramatic to me, but I couldn't fathom the depth of emotions she was experiencing.

"Emotion: disturbance of the mind, vehemence of passion," wrote Samuel Johnson.

Perhaps she assumed her mother might have died or fallen seriously ill, or she was overwhelmed by her own thoughts and unable to manage her emotions.

The weather was cold, but the beads of sweat were visible on her forehead. Everyone stared at her. She created a scene like a tragic *tamasa*, carnival. Krisha reached for her mother with determination, but I held her close to my chest, finding peace in the embrace. A profound sense of paternal emotion enveloped me, as I held my daughter and cherished the fulfillment of my dreams to be present for her. Despite the challenges and stresses accompanying the situation, I remained steadfast in my commitment to provide comfort and security to Krisha.

People thronged around and asked me, "What happened?" A few others gathered out of curiosity.

The security guard arrived and showed concern. One of the officials in uniform at the Buddha Air counter asked, "What happened to her?"

After explaining the situation, the request came plainly: "Can you please make two tickets available for us?"

The man behind the counter glanced from me to Kripa's tear-streaked face—and seemed to slip into *kimkartavyavimudh*, a Hamlet-like state of indecision and inner conflict.

"*Dai*, I would help you if I could. The plane is full, but if you please wait until noon, I will secure two seats for you at any cost."

He sympathized with our dilemma but stood firm in his response.

The mind couldn't make sense of anything—not fast enough to know what should come next.

"Shit," the word slipped out, tight and trembling.

The force of the moment struck without warning.

"Oh, God, help me."

Religious conviction had never been a defining trait, but in moments like these, even those who don't often pray reach out for something greater.

Two young men, likely in their late twenties, lingered near Kripa, their eyes on us.

After a moment of quiet observation, they stepped forward with an unexpected offer.

"*Dai*, we are also going to Pokhara on the nine o'clock flight. Please use our tickets, and we will go on a different flight at noon."

Gratitude surged toward them.

"Thank you so much, brothers," the words came with sincerity before returning to the counter to update and pay for the tickets.

With bags in hand and family beside me, we moved quickly through security. At the gate, the plane was nearly ready for departure.

We boarded and settled into our seats.

Krisha squirmed away from my lap, so I gently passed her to Kripa, who sat silently, her thoughts clearly fixed on her mother.

As the plane ascended, my eyes stayed on Krisha, making sure she remained safe in her mother's arms, while Kripa stared absently out the window.

A young lady with a pony tail was seated next to us.

"*Dai*, what happened to *didi*?" she asked.

"Her mother is sick in the hospital," I answered. "So, she is worried."

There was no point in sharing all the details with everyone. Despite their words of sympathy, they wouldn't care since this had nothing to do with their own immediate family members.

I remembered something my mother used to say.

"People are more willing to hear your laughter than your pain," she had said.

Although I tried to comfort Kripa and hide the deep fear inside me, my heart pounded against my ribs. I tried to put myself into Kripa's heart and head. *What if she discovered her mother had died? Would she be able to accept that?*

"*God, give her power to endure it,*" I thought.

My eyes were closed as I braced myself. Kripa gripped my right hand.

"*Budho*, I hope nothing is wrong with my mother. If anything— how can I live?"

"Why are you speaking rubbish, baby? Nothing has happened to your mother," I said. "She is in the hospital, in the hands of capable doctors. Don't worry too much. We will be there soon."

Her hands tightened around mine, and I rubbed her back gently in an effort to soothe.

Tears were wiped away once more.

"Why are you crying again? Please don't cry. See, your baby starts crying when she sees you in tears," the words came out pleading, though they carried the unintended weight of a scolding.

To comfort our daughter, I accepted a candy from the flight attendant—first biting it to show it was safe, then offering it to her with hope.

The young women beside us called softly to her, inviting her into their laps. For a few minutes, she accepted their distraction.

Emotion swelled at the sight of my wife's pain, but now wasn't the time to surrender to feeling—her needs came first.

Twenty-five minutes after takeoff, the plane landed in Pokhara.

Krisha and the bags stayed close in my arms, while Kripa clutched her small handbag.

As we descended the ladder, the propellers roared, wind rising around us, nearly deafening.

A sprint followed—toward the gate, toward whatever waited.

The moment the phone was switched back on, it rang.

Jaya *dai*.

"We brought our mother-in-law back from the hospital," he said. "You guys can come directly here from the airport."

As soon as he said it, the truth landed—*Sasuma* had likely already passed. Perhaps the hospital had done all it could and had sent her home.

Words failed—not just from personal sorrow, but from the empathy pressing in, the unbearable imagining of Kripa's pain.

The question of how to navigate what lay ahead sank deep, quiet and unrelenting.

That weight had to be hidden, tucked away to spare her from even more.

Fragile hope flickered in her eyes, "Who's calling?"

There was no way out.

Every answer felt like a betrayal. None would shield her from the truth.

If I said, "Your mother is home now. We shouldn't go to the hospital," it would only lead her to the unspoken conclusion—that her mother had died, or that nothing more could be done.

No clarity came. My mind spun between silence and truth.

Above us, clouds drifted by.

Birds cut through the sky.

A plane roared overhead.

I turned my eyes away.

"Why are you not talking to me?" she shouted. "Please tell me. What happened? My mother didn't die, did she?"

People turned to her with curious eyes, as if I had done something wrong to her. I held Krisha tightly in my arms.

"Why are you making unnecessary predictions before you reach the hospital?" The words came out firm, but gently, with care. "Jaya *dai* phoned me and said we shouldn't be scared. Let's focus on getting there. That's all that matters."

Bringing Kripa to her parents' house felt like the only option. Surely the people there would find ways to support her.

But watching her cry stirred something deeper—an ache, a helplessness that left everything inside unraveling.

There was no choice but to be strong.

The role demanded more than comfort; it required resolve.

Kripa's sobs finally faded into soft hiccups. For a moment, she held Krisha.

Outside the airport's main gate, the search for a taxi to Sisuwa began—the village where her parents lived, and where this sorrow now pointed us.

It was an unfortunate coincidence that Pokhara was closed. The city was located in the Kaski district, which was a tourist destination due to its scenic beauty and excursions like bungee jumping, paragliding, and boating.

It was closed for the election to replace Rabindra Adhikari, Nepal's tourism minister who had died in a plane crash a few weeks earlier. Rabindra's wife Bidhya Bhattarai was nominated as one of the candidates.

I hated that our politics were so dirty. When a male politician died prematurely, the party promoted his wife as the ideal candidate to represent the constituency where her husband had been elected. Such politics engulfed the country. Why did they have to close down during elections? Why did they interfere with everyday people's lives? *This is not more important than our grief,* I thought. In America, they didn't close the city or country. People continued with their daily chores unaffected.

Sisuwa was ten miles from the airport. Since there were no taxies or public vehicles on the road, I worried how we could make it home.

The walk back led to where Kripa sat with Krisha, two bags resting at her side.

"Today, Pokhara is closed due to the election," someone said. "No taxis are on the road."

Her eyes were red and swollen, with tear-streaks leaving raw trails across her cheeks.

No mention had yet been made of the plan to go to Sisuwa—she still believed the destination was Gandaki Hospital.

The search for a taxi continued, performed with the urgency of someone bound for the hospital, though the true intention was to head straight to her parents' home.

Since Kripa was a journalist by profession, she had many friends. She had upstanding public relations with locals and journalists. She called Ram Prasad Gyawali, editor-in-chief of Samadhan, a Nepali national daily newspaper, but he didn't answer the phone. So, she called another journalist friend, Tribhuvan Poudyal.

"Tribhuvan *jee*, my mother is seriously ill and has been hospitalized. Can you please give us a ride? You must know Pokhara is closed today and only journalists are allowed in. Can you please take me from the airport to the hospital?"

Listening to her quavering and anguished voice, he couldn't say no. He rushed to the airport and found his friend in tears.

Krisha and I sat in the backseat and Kripa in the front passenger seat. All the bags were inside the car with me. Tribhuvan was a young guy in his early thirties, ambitious, well dressed, his hair tossed back. Three years later he would die in a plane crash in Pokhara.

"Where would you like to go? Which hospital?" Tribhuvan asked.

"Gandaki Hospital," she said, trying to muffle her sobs.

He shifted the gear of his manual car and said nothing more.

The moment had come—there was no choice but to speak the truth.

"Not right now," came my quiet reply. "I received a call from Jaya *dai*. They've already brought her home, so we should go there."

Seated in the middle of the passenger seat, my eyes stayed fixed on the road through the windshield.

A quick correction came just in time for the driver to shift lanes.

Kripa guessed her mother was dead from my instructions.

"Mother, why are you there, why are you not in the hospital now? No, mother, no. You cannot leave me." She was inconsolable.

She cried and shrieked. I understood she needed to vent her emotions. Calming her with words didn't work. Tribhuvan continued driving, his focus unbroken.

"Why are you taking me home, *Budho*? Why?" she cried louder, as she hid her head in her hands.

I again felt helpless, speechless, not knowing how to answer her question. All my efforts to persuade and comfort were in vain.

"Why are you crying? What must happen will happen. We have not reached home yet. Our daughter is crying too. She is more scared. Please, darling, don't do this. I am praying for your mother's recovery. Maybe that's why the doctors released her. Try to control yourself. Do not make conjectures until we find the truth."

I knew all my efforts to console her were useless. The more I tried, the more she shrieked and yelled, "Drive faster!" Tribhuvan didn't dare peek at her, let alone console her.

Finally, Tribhuvan coughed twice and mustered the courage to speak.

"Kripa *jee,* your tears won't solve the problem. Let's reach home first and see how your mother is doing."

Both his hands were on the steering wheel and his eyes were on the road ahead.

Krisha and Kripa continued to cry, and I tried to carry them forward as a driver, not of the car, but of our love and relationship. I prayed she would find the strength to survive her pain.

The bond she shared with her mother was more special than any other mother-daughter duo I'd seen—deeper and more emotional. Her emotional attachment with her mother was so strong because she'd spent most of her time with her mother, who tended her needs as a child. Her mother worked hard and struggled a lot to support her children, forbidding them from doing any work for the sake of their happiness. She hid all the pain and pangs behind a smile.

"I love my mother more than my own life. If anything happens to her, I will go insane. I will die," Kripa said. "The only person I can trust in this world is my mother, who worked dawn to dusk to support us, to make sure we received an education. She spent money on us instead of buying new clothes to replace her ragged ones. Our happy lives were her joy and satisfaction. My father was not around most of the time. She played the role of mother and father while he was working outside the country when we were toddlers."

Tribhuvan stopped the car in the courtyard of the house where a throng of neighboring people had gathered. The sights and sounds of wailing were apparent. As soon as Kripa saw the commotion, she opened the car door and walked straight into the crowd, wailing and grunting, she joined them shrieking and crying out loud. The crowd had besieged the dead body of Kripa's mother, who was lying flat on the pavement next to the house.

She hugged the dead body of her mother and shrieked, "Mother!"

She was unaware of anything around her except her feelings toward her mother. She was devastated. She could only think of her mother; not her husband, nor her daughter. Her world was empty, destroyed. Krisha reacted with her own cries. Still in my arms—perhaps she wondered what was going on, why her mother didn't respond to her cries. She finally stopped crying and gazed at the frightening crowd of people, most of whom had cried, but were now wiping their eyes.

One of the villagers came to me and took my daughter from me.

"I will take care of her."

I thought she must be the right person, and I let Krisha go with her, although she was not comfortable going with a stranger. I had to help my wife. Kripa's mother was dead, and next to her body were Suman *didi* and my mother-in-law's youngest sister. She had been weeping for hours and trying to revive her mother.

"Please wake up. You can't leave us," she repeated as if in a trance.

After my wife joined them and embraced her mother's lifeless body, their sobs rose again, tears streaking down their cheeks. I turned away, unable to bear the sight. My heart splintered. I fled to a corner and let the wave crash over me, wiping tears from my face with the heel of my palm. Grief welled up, too heavy to name, too dense to cry out.

I didn't want to see, but I heard Kripa saying, "My mother, please come back to life. I need you to come back. Don't make me a half-orphan. Now who is left in this world for me, to love me, to think of me, to take care of me? Mother, come back."

Seeing her collapse under the weight of the news, I felt something crack open in me. A mother is everything.

I thought of my own mother—how she rose before the sun, worked long hours in other people's fields before we had land of our own, and still made sure we were fed and sent to school. Her strength was quiet but unshakable. Because of her, I became the man who now teaches at a university in America.

She rarely ate enough, hardly slept, and never complained. She kept going. For us.

There's a line by Victor Hugo I once read: *"A mother's arms are made of tenderness, and children sleep soundly in them."* I had always liked the quote, but now, watching Kripa lose her mother, it sank in with new weight.

I also remembered a scene from *Sunyako Mulya* (*The Price of Zero*)—a video described in the book, where a mother deer sacrifices herself to save her fawn from a crocodile. That moment had stunned the world. But this—this was Kripa's world breaking open in front of me.

Gazing at the dead body of her mother, she screamed so loudly death itself would run in terror. If her tears were rain, they would have washed the crowd away in the flood. At the death of the most important person in her life, Kripa's wailing almost felt unreal, like a scene from a tragedy. The line between reality and drama was blurred.

"Mother, please open your eyes. I have come here to be with you. See me."

She continued wailing as if she had gone mad. She shoved at her mother's body and scanned the crowd.

"See, do you see that? She opened her eyes. Someone, help me. My mother is not dead. We must get her back to the hospital. Call the doctor. See, see? My mother opened her eyes."

When I saw my love in such a state and heard her words of mad grief, my head whirled and a heavy weight settled in my chest. If her pain were the waves of the ocean, they would drown the village a thousand miles away. If her shrieking and wailing were thunder, it would destroy the whole neighborhood. But none of it would bring her mother back to life.

Finally, she joined the procession to the crematorium on the banks of the Seti River. Both she and her sister Suman gave her mother a *Dagbatti*. Upon seeing her swathed in grief and courage, the fire that engulfed her mother's body might have feared her.

After we returned from the crematorium, Kripa saw her mother's photo on the living room wall—and collapsed.

I rushed to her side and caught her just before she hit the floor.

"Please! Someone, help!" I shouted. "What's happening to my wife?"

She was limp in my arms, and panic surged through me. I couldn't think—only hold her, afraid of what I didn't understand. My vision blurred. Sweat ran down my brow. The room tilted.

Someone brought water and gently sprinkled it on her face.

"Darling, please don't do this," I whispered, gripping her hand. "Everything will be alright. Stay with me."

As soon as she gained consciousness, she went to the cupboard and took out all the clothes her mother used to wear and hugged them.

"This is my mother's most favorite *sari*."

She raised the cloth up like a precious symbol.

"All my happiness and joys were brought up in the hems of this garment. She gardened my dreams, watered my aspirations. What else didn't you do for me, mother, for the sake of my contentment? You spent many cold seasons making sure I had enough warmth. Countless nights you went hungry, making sure I was full. I complained. I got so angry a great deal. But you never shouted at me. You always spoke to me with a smile on your face. You never showed me your pain. You remained gentle, always loving and caring. We had started harvesting the fruit of our lives, but you've left us for forever. Why, mother, why? It's not fair. What is the point of my dream, our dreams? What meaning does my life hold?"

Kripa clutched her mother's *sari*, murmuring to herself, lost in her grief. We let her speak, let her cry. The room was quiet except for her voice and the sound of sobs.

She wept until no more tears came—until the wetness dried on her cheeks.

In the corner, Suman *didi* cried alone. Visitors hovered at the doorway, unsure whether to step inside.

Across the room, my father-in-law sat on a traditional *chowki*—a wooden bed close to the floor that is common in Nepali homes—surrounded by neighbors trying to console him. But his eyes were vacant. His face twisted under the weight of something too heavy for words. He hugged his stomach, as if trying to keep the heartache from spilling out.

Today he was meant to be in Kathmandu. Instead, he sat in a house full of sorrow, with a body that betrayed him and a sorrow that wouldn't let go.

Watching him, I felt the weight of it too—a pain without a clear origin spreading through me like a sickness I couldn't name.

Grief, I learned, didn't need us to do anything. It needed space. Tears carried what words couldn't.

And over time—hours, not moments—Kripa's sobs softened. The room held her distress until it had somewhere to go.

By nighttime, she had found ways to comfort herself. The tears had rolled down her cheeks and helped wash away the unendurable anguish. I brought Krisha back from the neighbor and handed her to Kripa, who started to breastfeed.

Does she see her mother's image in our child? I wondered. I got lost in the scene of mother and child, which filled me with relief. I finally felt a small spark of hope and optimism.

Chapter Two

Memories

May 10, 2018

My *sasuma* gardened on the top floor, watered the plants and cleared the weeds in the evening. In the north, the snow-clad Machhapuchhre and Annapurna mountains were glazed in the setting sun's golden hue. She planted many types of produce—bitter gourd, pumpkins, beans, and green leafy vegetables—and plants like the Makhamali flower, Gomphrena.

"The chickens roaming around stunted the growth of the leafy greens. They constantly peck at the leaves," she complained, sending them to the coop on the same floor.

She enjoyed doing one job after another, always with a smile on her face, never showing any exhaustion. Her forehead glistened with beads of sweat. It was my third visit to my *sasuma's* house and she was always warm and welcoming.

"*Jwaisaap*, son-in-law, you might be hungry," she said as she continued to garden. "The food will be ready in no time."

"Don't worry, mother. I am full. Kripa made me plenty of noodle soup half an hour ago," I said as I watched her machine-like movements.

Kripa was showing me the different sides of Pokhara and other lakes from the top floor, pointing to everything with her finger.

"There lies Dipang Lake. You see all the way to the east, on the top of the hill? That is Rupakot."

"Did you really feed *Jwai* noodle soup?" my *sasuma* asked Kripa.

She wiped sweat from her forehead with one finger. A drop fell on the leaf of a taro plant and remained there like morning dew.

"Yes, I did, but it is time to cook dinner anyway," Kripa said and hugged me from behind. "Do you want me to cook?"

"No, I will do everything. You be with *Jwai*," my *sasuma* said and went downstairs to the kitchen.

We hung out for a few minutes on the top floor.

"What isn't possible if you work hard?" Kripa said, playing with the stripes on the T-shirt I was wearing. "I don't want to brag about anything, nor do have I such attitudes. I am proud of my parents for giving me high moral values and principled culture. We are people of simple means."

"Thank you for sharing that with me," I said as I played with her hair and gazed at the glistening hills in the north.

"From the money they earned from the restaurant, they bought a small amount of land where they established their tea stand, and, finally, managed to build a three-story house ten years after they had started the business," she said, indicating the house we stood in. "Now, a twenty-five-foot road runs along both sides of the house, and the first floor has two store shutters that they've rented out." She spoke with confidence, optimism, and happiness.

My in-laws' house was in Sisuwa Chowk, in the Lekhnath Municipality of Pokhara. Twenty-five years ago, they had started with a humble tea stand, later transforming it into a small restaurant.

"Customers thronged there as soon as we opened," Kripa said, her eyes bright. "My parents had a knack for making people feel welcome."

I could almost hear her father's voice as she spoke: *I cared more about my clients than money. If you focus on service rather than what you'll gain, success will find you.*

"That's a powerful way to live," I'd once told him.

Kripa nudged me, pulling me back to the present. I drew her close, my arms and attention around her.

"Maybe we should open a business ourselves," I said. "Put your parents' wisdom to work for us, huh?"

"If push comes to shove," she agreed. "Of course. They always brought us up like we were the sons in the family, not restricting us to kitchen chores."

There was a lot of truth in Kripa's words. My in-laws had two daughters, no sons. And yet I never heard them raise their voices. I was always impressed by their intelligence, friendliness, and gentleness. They were always willing to listen to me with a smile on their face. When I visited them, my *sasuma* frequently asked Kripa if I wanted anything or if I was hungry or if I was okay. She worked on her own and never asked her daughters for a helping hand.

"Didn't your father want to have a son, which every Nepali family prefers over a daughter?" I asked.

"That's true. Because there wasn't a boy in the house, our community kept pressuring my father to marry another wife so he could, but my father didn't listen to them. If he wanted, he could have had another child from my mother or could have married another woman to have a son in the family, but he didn't," Kripa said. "That's why I admire and respect my father. My father is like an ocean of kindness. He would never notice himself going broke if he gave all his things away to the poor."

Kripa's sister Suman, the eldest, lived in Pokhara with her husband Jaya and their two children—Zenith, ten, and Araju, three. She ran a small business that sold all things related to sewing—cloth, thread, and needles. They lived modestly, but well enough.

On paper, Kripa's life read like a success story. With my job in the U.S.—the dream destination for most Nepalis—and her work as a journalist, we had financial stability. We owned a house in Kathmandu, something many could only imagine.

For a moment, I believed in that life. That we had made it. But as I stood in the thick of grief, it all felt fragile.

Could this perfect life be an illusion? One built by people like us, encouraged by a government that kept all opportunity tied to Kathmandu. The fantasy of a better life had driven people from their villages, left parents behind, and convinced us proximity to power was the same as peace.

Still, I remembered my in-laws sometimes looking at me with pride. "We are lucky to have a wonderful son-in-law like you," they'd say. And for a moment, I had believed them.

Kripa surveyed the hills as she reflected on her mother's struggles.

"My mother managed without a man in the house for many years," she said, her voice steady but laced with emotion.

She shifted slightly, her fingers fidgeting with the hem of her shirt.

"My father was often away for work. In a society that expects a man's presence, it wasn't easy for her."

She glanced down, the memories pressing in. "Working at a tea stand and looking after us while handling male customers was tough. Her only emotional support was rooted in her love for us and the joy she found in our smiles."

"I'm in awe of her," I remarked, taking in the strength behind her words. The shadows around us deepened as the hills to the north vanished from view, swallowed by the encroaching darkness.

"It's getting dark," Kripa said, her tone shifted as she glanced toward the stairs. We began to descend, the sounds of motorcycles and tractors whizzing by outside, their honking horns and bright beams cutting through the gloom. The atmosphere felt heavy with the weight of her mother's sacrifices, but also filled with a quiet resilience that echoed in Kripa's spirit.

We came downstairs to the living room where my *sasuraba*, was watching TV.

"Hey, Gita, are you not done with dinner?" he asked as if he were his wife's boss. "I am hungry. Did you get lost?"

"Cooking," she said from the kitchen in her soft and kind voice. "Will be ready soon."

"Mother, do you need help?"

Kripa rose and moved toward the other room as she spoke.

"No, no, you don't have to. Be with *Jwai*. I will take care of everything," she said.

She was happy and excited to work independently and serve her family.

I walked across the corridor of the house and found my *sasuma* cooking goat meat. A wave of spices hit the air—earthy, sharp, rich with chilies and garlic—and my mouth watered instantly. She dropped the chopped vegetables into the wok, and the crackle of frying filled the room. When she turned on the tap and nothing came out, she grabbed a *gagri* (an earthen pot) and headed downstairs, calling for Kripa to watch the vegetables so they wouldn't dry out. Outside the temple, she found another source and came back with a full bucket.

"I could have brought it," Kripa said. "Why must you do everything?"

"This is nothing. I am fine. You be with *Jwai*," she said with the same smile. The bangles on her wrists clinked delightfully together. "You don't have to. Go sit next to your husband who might feel lonely without you around."

I continuously heard my *sasuma's* bangles as she washed dishes, swept the floor, and sprinted around to do other house chores.

"She will help you, mother. Why are you doing everything on your own?" I added.

"I enjoy it, *Jwai*," she said as she arranged and fixed things. "You are here for a day or a two. After that you will go to your own house. Or will you leave her here for us?"

In no time, she finished cooking the rice, goat meat, lentil soup, beans, vegetables, pickled tomatoes, and leafy greens. She took out the plates from the rack, cleaned and wiped them, and served food to three of us: my *sasuraba*, me and Kripa.

She said, "Please eat there and relax with the TV on."

The room held an old sixteen-inch television, its screen coated in dust from the road outside. The green carpet had faded with time, its surface worn and stained, though someone had clearly swept it recently. A thick pillar stood awkwardly in the middle of the space, blocking the view for anyone sitting behind it.

By the door, a *chowki* bed faced two queen-sized ones. The yellow paint on the walls peeled from several spots, with patches of water damage showing through like scars.

And yet, the room was full of life—echoing with voices, laughter, and the scent of cooking. What it lacked in design, it made up for in warmth and the quiet presence of a family held together by care.

"Mother, you also need to come join us," I said, sitting cross-legged on the floor in preparation for the meal.

"I will, soon," she said. She waited until we finished eating before asking, "Do you want anything else?"

The food was so delicious I added a little of everything. She made many trips from the kitchen to the living room, back and forth. I felt guilty watching her, but she was radiant with joy.

After we finished, she finally ate on her own. She was happy with her own way of doing things, glad to serve and work. She didn't let Kripa wash the dishes or clean up the kitchen.

She said, "I never asked you for these things when you lived with me. I did everything on my own, and that is how we have spent many years. Now you live with your husband and come here to visit me for a day or two. Why should you do them now? This is my daily routine, and I am happy with it. If I can see your face, it's enough for me."

By the time she finished doing everything and got ready for bed, it was ten o'clock. She came to the living room where *Sasuraba* had already fallen asleep on the couch.

"Now is my time to speak with *Jwai*," she said with a smile and sat down next to Kripa, who was by my side in bed.

"Perhaps *Jwai* is tired too. Let him rest, put some oil on his feet and give him a massage so he will sleep well," my *sasuma* said and went into the kitchen again to bring some mustard oil.

"I don't need it," I replied.

My *sasuma* massaged Kripa's legs and Kripa massaged my legs, but poor *Sasuma's* feet never got a massage, despite working harder than anyone else.

My eyes shut and I drifted into a soft and dreamless slumber.

Chapter Three

Branch of an Uprooted Tree

December 1, 2019

What difference would someone's death make to the continuity of days and nights?

The question popped into my head. Each day had twenty-four hours, divided into day and night, and the night of my mother-in-law's death was like any other. The only difference was that my mother-in-law was not breathing. Her physical body was burned to ashes at the banks of the Seti River, which had already carried them away with its current. The only thing that remained was her smiling picture hanging on the living room wall, and the memories she left behind. Everything was transient; nothing was permanent. Memories would one day disappear.

My *sasuraba* sat on a red couch in the living room, his face sad and somber, staring out at the verandah. He no longer expressed his typical sense of humor he usually had during our meetings. Shoulders slumped; hands limp on his knees—his strength gone.

"How did the incident happen?" I mustered the courage to ask him.

"In the morning, my wife and I left the house to go to Kathmandu for my treatment. I was walking slowly ahead of my wife. When I didn't see her after a while, I turned around and found her lying on the road a few meters back," he said with his eyes tearful and looked up at the ceiling. "I called Laxman *bhanja*, who brought her to the hospital, but she had already stopped breathing. None of us were sure about the actual cause of her death, but according to Laxman *bhanja*, the doctor said it was because of a heart attack."

I lacked the bravery to reply or find the right words to console him while he grieved the loss of his wife.

He was also in serious physical pain, had lost his appetite, was suffering from a stomach ailment. His two daughters Kripa and Suman had to remain in a closed, secluded area as part of their mourning ritual, which would continue for thirteen days. Neighbors helped them maintain their seclusion.

"Now we have to go to Kathmandu for your treatment," I said.

"I am worried about Kripa and Suman," he added. "They don't have brothers for support during the grieving time. How can I leave them in such a state until the lamenting is over?"

"Why fret over that?" I reassured him. "The nearby residents will handle it. That's one of the wonderful aspects of Nepali society. During occasions like weddings, births, and funerals, people come together to lend a helping hand if necessary."

"Yes, but if I'm here, I can at least guide them and ensure the tasks are accomplished successfully," he replied, his hand pressed against his stomach, wincing in pain. "At least my wife in heaven will know we executed all the responsibilities following her passing with utmost finesse."

"Would you like to drink tea, Father?" I couldn't argue with his logic, so I decided to change the subject. I felt a cough tickling my throat. I cleared it, forcing it out.

"Leave it for now. Someone will make it later," he said.

His eyes were wet. He pressed his stomach with his hand again, trying in vain to lessen the pain. He was supposed to be seeing the doctor in Kathmandu, but due to the untimely and accidental death of his wife, he had to wait until we could reschedule another appointment.

"You must see the doctor as soon as possible, father," I said.

Grief passed across his face like a shadow.

"What is the point of living after I've lost my beloved anyway?" he asked. "When she was around, I never had to do anything except eat and chat with friends and people in town, especially after I became sick. She used to bring food to my bed, wash my hands, and help me with my medicines despite all her kitchen chores and shopping."

I remained tight-lipped with my eyes pressed closed.

"I never bothered to ask if she had eaten while she was feeding me all the time," he added, his eyes brimming with tears. "Perhaps I never knew how to express my love, or it was the culture I lived in that didn't allow me to express my feelings toward my spouse explicitly."

I grasped his hands gently, sandwiching them between mine, and began to caress them. The fragile skin with prominent veins resembled delicate lines on a sheet of paper. They were worn, dry, and pallid in appearance.

I could see in his face the terrible loss he had suffered. I could see how much he missed her. Perhaps he was wondering who would offer the warmth and care of a wife once his daughters returned to their own homes. No matter how much they tried to be there for him, it would never compare to the comfort he had once known. A deep helplessness settled over me.

"She always prepared medicine and handed me the right amount at the right time along with a glass of water to swallow the pills," he continued, in lachrymose tones. "She prepared the insulin to inject in my belly for years now. If I didn't see her around, I would shout to her and ask where she was. Now who will listen to my anxieties and frustrations? Who can I shout at? Who will take care of me and understand my feelings?

"Gita did everything for me," he continued in a stream of consciousness. "She was the one to keep the house and the children when I was not around. My only job was to demand a cooked meal when I was hungry. She made it right away. She always knew how to make things the way I liked them. None of my daughters are capable of doing it. Gita never taught them what to do in the kitchen."

A dryness crept into my throat as I listened to him. I drank water from a bottle nearby and replied, "I hear you, father. I can see you are feeling pain in your stomach. No matter what, we should go to Kathmandu for treatment as soon as possible."

"Let it be. The tree has been uprooted. What is the point of the branch of an uprooted tree?"

His words made me lift one side of my T-shirt and wipe my eyes.

Visitors came and went. Some swept the floors, others stirred pots in the kitchen or wiped down dusty corners. A few sat with the mourners, murmuring the usual questions: "What can we do when so little is in our control?"

Outside, life moved on. Motorcycles and buses rumbled down the road, horns echoing through the walls. The temple bells kept ringing. Laughter drifted from the women at the tap beside the shrine.

Suman and Kripa had already bathed and sat apart in the space designated for their thirteen days of mourning. Krisha played nearby with *Fupudidi*, her grandfather's sister, who had taken on the task of caring for her. Kripa would only hold her daughter when it was time to breastfeed or put her to sleep.

We kept our distance. No one was allowed to touch the mourners, for fear of making them impure. Still, I needed to ask about her father's condition, and whether I should take him to Kathmandu.

She and Suman sat on hay spread across the floor, with a foam pad for warmth. Wrapped in shawls and blankets, their hair uncombed, worn and untouchable—grieving in silence. Their loose, unstitched clothes spoke of ritual. But their faces spoke of loss.

For a moment, the scene reminded me of a Greek tragedy—like something from Sophocles, where fate crashes in and leaves nothing whole.

Kripa and Suman *didi's* eyes were swollen. Helpless, as if they had lost everything and were wondering how to begin life again, life without their mother. Seeing them in such a state, I didn't know what to say.

"Your father is suffering from severe stomach pain. What can we do? When do you think we can bring him to Kathmandu?" I blurted out while rubbing both hands in discomfort. They could at least find comfort if their father was healthy, but they had lost courage and confidence because of his ailing condition.

"We should take him to the hospital in Kathmandu as soon as possible," Kripa said, trying to wrap herself up. She stuck her tongue out and dampened her dry lips.

Trying to sit cross-legged next to Kripa, Suman *didi* said, "Please talk to other relatives around and ask for help bringing him to Kathmandu. My father doesn't have to live in a secluded place, nor does he have to mourn without eating salty food. We have people here to help. Jaya can care for us so you can take him to Kathmandu."

Nepali culture could be so bizarre at times. When a husband died, the wife had to mourn for thirteen days, dress in white clothing for almost a year, and remain unmarried for the rest of her life. But when the wife died, the husband had no mourning obligations.

"You and Laxman *dai* can take *Buwa* in Laxman *dai's* car," Kripa chimed in. "Wait, I will also talk to him when he gets here."

"Sure," I said. "Let's do it as soon as possible, today or tomorrow."

I went upstairs to the living room where my father-in-law was sitting. His cousins stood around him, talking to him. I had never seen them before. My *sasuraba* introduced me as his youngest son-in-law. Since I was living in America when I had come to Nepal for the marriage, I spent only two weeks with the immediate family, which didn't give me time to visit Kripa's relatives.

I listened to the relatives' conversations.

"This is shocking! Did she have any sickness or disease?" one of the men asked, removing his *topi* (Nepali cap) and scratching his head. A long grey pigtail dangled from the center of his bald scalp. He put the *topi* back on.

"No. She was fine. She had been looking after me, feeding me, caring for me, taking me to the doctor," my *sasuraba* answered, his mouth pressed tightly in pain. He pushed his right hand to his stomach again and again.

Another relative murmured that what had happened should not have happened. Nothing was under one's control. He echoed the shared feeling among those gathered. A story followed, saliva appearing at the corners of his mouth. "My uncle's wife also died the same way. She was walking and fell on the road, and she died before anyone managed to lift her up and bring her to the hospital. We never know what kind of ailments exist inside our bodies. We don't know when death will come and take us away."

Then a cousin chimed in, stroking his long and thick moustache with his right hand. "How can you live like this without a wife? Now you need someone to take care of you. Perhaps you need to marry another woman."

I couldn't believe what I was hearing. The words made my jaw tighten. Her body was barely cold, and he was already being encouraged to replace her.

I remembered what Kripa had once told me—how people had pressured her father to marry again to try for a son. The same cold calculation was behind this comment, too. Not grief. Not care.

Was he worried about who would inherit the land? With no son, it would go to the daughters. Did that not sit well with him?

It made me sick.

"Your wife did a lot of outstanding things in her life. Perhaps that was why she died without any pain. She just fell and died," someone in the group said and sneezed openly in the air, spreading germs around without apology.

Nepali people don't often verbalize apologies the way people in America do, where it's typical to say excuse me or sorry. I had grown used to this cultural difference and often took it for granted.

Laxman *dai* entered the room. He was a man of around fifty. Short. Plump. His belly protruded a bit.

"*Jwaisaap*, what is the condition of your father-in-law?" he asked as soon as he entered the room. Laxman was the son of my *sasuraba's* sister. "Do you think we can take him to Kathmandu for a treatment? I already talked to Kripa and Suman." It was ten in the morning.

"I am ready to do it. Let's go," I said, standing up from the edge of the bed where I was sitting.

"No, we can't go today. We have to sort out the division of work here," my Sasuraba said while holding his stomach with one of his hands and grimacing. "Let's go early tomorrow and, if possible, we can return home the same day."

"What's the rush, father?" I asked my *sasuraba*, walking into the room. "We can stay at my house in Kathmandu. We must focus on your treatment. You have nothing to do here. We have Jaya *dai* and others to handle everything. First, we need to make sure that we completely cure your ailment."

"Fine. If the doctor wants us to stay, I won't refuse," he said. "You are like my son. Why should I worry?"

Something in the warmth of his voice settled my nerves. In that moment, despite everything, I felt seen—trusted.

We planned to leave Pokhara for Kathmandu early the next morning.

Chapter Four

Humans, Rivers, and the Tears of Mountains

December 2, 2019

Around six in the morning, we were ready to go to Kathmandu for my *sasuraba's* treatment. Laxman *dai* started his car's engine to warm it up in the morning chill, then he called us to come down from the house. My father-in-law and Laxman *dai* were like friends, always together for years. They helped each other. They built two houses twenty-five years ago, like a duplex, but they kept each property separate, in their own names. The age difference between them was eleven years, meaning my father-in-law was sixty-three and Laxman *dai* was fifty.

In their secluded room, Kripa and Suman were still sleeping. After letting Jaya *dai* know we were leaving for Kathmandu, we got into Laxman *dai's* vehicle.

"You can sit in the passenger seat here in the back and relax," Laxman *dai* said, opening the door for my *sasuraba* and pointing to the pillow he'd placed there. "You can use that to rest. You can also sleep if you want to. We'll be up front."

I opened the front door and slid into the passenger seat.

"Sure," my father-in-law said.

He nodded at both of us as he tried to climb in. His hands shook as if he were inebriated, his eyes pale and sunken.

"*Jwai*, did you manage to bring along all my previous doctors' documents?" he asked, his voice trembling.

"I did, *Buwa*," I replied, glancing back at him. "I put all those documents in my backpack last night."

"We should stop for petrol up ahead," Laxman *dai* said, adjusting his seat, mirrors, and steering wheel. He sneezed, coughed, and wrapped himself in his muffler.

"Sure."

My father-in-law was already stretched out in the back with the pillow under his head. Laxman *dai* started the engine, and we pulled away. The temperature hovered around sixty degrees Fahrenheit, and the area was foggy. The Sisuwa region was often misty in the mornings, especially in winter, but today the fog was denser than usual.

At the petrol station, Laxman *dai* filled the tank.

"Now, we'll be able to make it back, too," he said, starting the engine once more.

"Won't we need to stop for fuel when we get there—or on the way back?" I asked, clicking the buckle across my chest. Though seatbelt use wasn't required in Nepal except for the driver, the habit had stayed with me after years of living in the United States. It felt safer that way.

"If we end up driving around Kathmandu, we might need to top it off," the driver replied, rolling down the window, spitting something out, and cranking it shut again.

The distance from Pokhara to Kathmandu was about one hundred fifty miles, but potholes and heavy traffic made it feel much farther. He kept shifting gears, grinding through the narrow, uneven roads. The trip would take a toll—on both fuel and time.

I glanced toward the back. *Sasuraba* was already asleep, gently snoring, his eyelids soft and still.

As Laxman *dai* drove, he brought up the topic of my mother-in-law's death.

"*Jwaisaap.* What a coincidence! As soon as you came from America, *Maiju* passed away the next day. It is beyond my imagination, beyond what one could think of," Laxman *dai* said.

He spoke while looking ahead on the road, both hands on the steering wheel. The innumerable curves along the edge of dangerous hills would be coming up, and he would drive on winding roads until we reached Kathmandu. He had a comfortable cushion and back support in his seat.

When I had pointed out the cushion earlier, he had told me, "This is the thing my son-in-law brought me from America. I find you exactly like him, and he is like you too." Laxman *dai* liked to talk and, at the same time, appreciated the compliment. I liked him as he appeared to be candid. I continued to admire him.

"It is tragic, *dai*. Death is so cruel! She was turning fifty-three—such a young age to die. Death snatched her away from all of us," I said, staring at the steering wheel where Laxman *dai* clenched his hands. By that time, we had arrived in Kotre, another small town on the way to Kathmandu.

"*Jwaisaap*, I usually step out around four in the morning. There are five of us who go together. We head north and meet at Ban Pokhari Danda. By the time we reach it, it's about six o'clock, and then we head home. I rest, take a shower, drink a glass of lemon water, and after a short nap, I eat wheat bread with a glass of milk. That's my daily routine," Laxman *dai* said, adjusting his grip on the steering wheel and tapping it like a *Tabala*, producing a rhythmic *tap-tap* and a soft *thch...thch* sound with his mouth.

My eyes drifted to his protruding belly, which didn't quite match the claim of two hours of morning exercise. I smiled to myself, quietly impressed by his discipline.

I remembered his hard work when my mother-in-law died—cutting bamboo and making a stretcher for the body, directing and advising people, setting things up and managing all the materials needed for the cremation. "Let's get things done on time," he had ordered the people around him.

Laxman kept his eyes on the road as he spoke.

He had been in the shower when the call came. He rushed out, still covered in soap, barely wiping himself down with a towel. There was no time to think.

It was six forty in the morning. He didn't bother to warm the engine—just lifted Maiju into the car and headed straight for Gandaki Hospital. What usually took thirty minutes, he drove in twenty. He never slowed down.

At the ER, the doctors checked her pulse. Nothing. She had been gone long before they arrived.

He gripped the steering wheel tighter, like he was still trying to hold on to her.

Curiosity overcame me, prompting me to ask about the condition in which he found her. He described a chilling sensation; her heart might still have been beating, but her hands and feet were ice-cold, lifeless.

Outside, thick fog blurred the windshield, and he switched on the wipers to clear his view. He coughed, rolled down the window to spit out some phlegm, rolled it back up, his actions mechanical, almost detached.

I pondered the grim possibility she might have died en route, and the weight of it lingered in every breath. In the rearview mirror, I caught a glimpse of my father-in-law. He lay against the seat, quiet and somber, absorbing our conversation, grief palpable in the air.

"Are you in pain?" I asked. "Is your stomach acting up again?"

"Let it be," he said. "That's why we're headed to the doctor. If you see a stand on the way, let's stop. I could use something warm."

I knew his craving—he needed milk *chai* at least three or four times a day. It was as regular as breath.

By the time we reached Damauli, the mist had begun to lift, peeling back the quiet of the morning. At the *chowk*, the town was waking up—vendors opened their stalls, steam curling into the cool air. People gathered in small circles, sipping and talking.

Women waited at the public tap, filling containers for the day ahead. Buses grumbled at the station. Stray dogs wove through the street, and a rooster let out a hoarse cry behind a food stall, cutting through the stillness.

"Let's make a quick stop at one of these," Laxman *dai* said, nodding toward a roadside vendor, coughing again as if the cold air didn't agree with him. We parked and stepped out.

"What breakfast do you have, *didi*?" I asked, approaching a woman stirring chickpeas in a large wok. She wore a threadbare *sari* and blouse; her face marked with the creases of a hard life. "Do you serve *chai*?"

"Yes, yes," she replied, smiling at us with anticipation. "I'm also cooking chickpeas, and they'll be ready in no time."

I turned to my father-in-law, who had settled onto a nearby bench.

"*Buwa*, what would you like to eat? The fresh chana is cooking now."

He nodded approvingly.

I then asked Laxman *dai* if he wanted something as well.

"We still have a long way to go. Let's grab a bite before we get hungry," he replied, clapping his hands eagerly for breakfast.

Laxman *dai* and my father-in-law enjoyed a plate of chickpeas and tea each, while I opted for a glass of tea, as Kripa had asked me not to consume salty food for at least five days.

"This tea is excellent," my father-in-law said, and we all agreed. I paid the bill.

"Brother, let me pay. It doesn't feel right for you to cover everything," Laxman *dai* said, reaching for his wallet.

I lifted a hand to stop him and handed the vendor one hundred fifty rupees—about one dollar and fifty cents. The price barely registered in American terms, but here, it meant more. In a place where some families survived on less than one hundred dollars a month, a cup of tea carried weight far beyond its cost.

We returned to the car and continued our journey, leaving Damauli Bazaar behind. If it were any other day, I would have asked Laxman *dai* to play a pleasant song in the car. But today, we were not in the mood. The days and nights passed as always. Though my mother-in-law had died only two days ago, I couldn't help but think about it—her untimely demise.

My mother-in-law had cared for Krisha during her first year, while Kripa worked in Pokhara and lived with her parents. *Sasuma* did everything—held the baby, cooked for the family, tended to her ailing husband—and never once complained.

I remembered how she used to wave off my concern.

"*Jwai*, don't worry about all this," she'd say, covering her mouth with a shawl or her hand. "It's nothing compared to what we went through in the early days. We're happy to have you as our *jwai*."

She had lost her front teeth and always tried to hide her smile—until she finally went to the dentist and had them fixed.

That memory undid me. I sat there, stunned. Silent tears slipped down my cheeks, and a wave of dizziness rose in my chest. I still couldn't believe she was gone.

"Don't you think the doctor could have simply touched her wrist and confirmed she was dead? Did you double check with the doctor?" I asked Laxman *dai*, as if I was not believing in what he said earlier.

"*Jwaisaap*, what are you talking about? The doctor has given me the EKG report, and all the records and papers are with me," he said, pointing out all the documents on the dashboard. "Here they are."

He pulled them out and handed them to me. I went through the papers and found the EKG report was blank. There was no heartbeat at all.

We passed by the building of Marshyangdi Water Electricity Planning. Laxman *dai* continued driving along the edge of the Marshyangdi River which would merge with the Trishuli River. Muglin Bazaar was situated at the junction of these two rivers—the Bazaar would diverge into two roads, one leading to Chitawan and the other to Kathmandu.

"Some people say if the heart stops, it can be restarted by using an electric shock in the person's body. Not sure how true it is, but could we have done that?" I said, perhaps sounding silly.

"*Jwaisaap*, how can the dead come back to life? The doctor did everything in his power but couldn't bring her back, so he let us go home. Do you think he only touched Maiju's hands and decided she was dead? Oh no!" he responded, as if mad at me for not believing him. His face flushed, and deep wrinkles gathered on his forehead.

"It is hard to digest the truth that she is dead. I talked to her a few days ago when I was in Kathmandu, the day I came from America. She had told me she would come and meet me in Kathmandu, and we hung up the phone. It is unbelievable. Death doesn't come ringing a bell to let us know," I said.

I tried to accept what he said while making sure what he was saying was right. I checked on my father-in-law in the back. He had fallen asleep again. We arrived at Kurintar's cable car station after passing Mungling. It was still early morning.

"Yes, death indeed is a bizarre thing. Nobody knows when it comes and plucks a person's life away. Maiju was not ill, either. I always saw her working—fit and fine. I never heard her complain of a headache, nor did I see her taking any over-the-counter medicine, like paracetamol. She always had a smile and a gentle tone of voice. She was a kind person in everyone's eyes; she never hurt anybody else's feelings," Laxman *dai* said, his voice breaking. He continued, "She had started enjoying her days. Her days of joy were approaching after her two daughters had gotten married. They found dependable husbands, like you—wise, educated, and understanding. But then all of a sudden, she died. What to say! It was meant to be her last day on earth." He took a deep, tired breath, as if he were carrying a heavy load on his back, and he adjusted himself in the seat.

Listening to him, my eyes filled with water. I stealthily pulled my jacket to the side and wiped my tears, but more returned immediately. My gaze wandered as I watched the comings and goings of cable cars on the hilltops. The Trishuli River was flowing along the side of the road where our car was moving. The hills were the same as always.

I thought: *The dead wouldn't make a bit of difference to these hills and mountains. In joy, we had been spoiled. We were not to cry in pain, not make promises in joy, not make quick decisions in anger. We were meant to be like the peaked ranges—determined and brave.*

My phone rang, and I saw it was Kripa calling. She asked where I was. I told her I had passed Kurintar and asked if everything was okay.

I ended the call and stared out the window, unsettled by Kripa's voice. It had been flat—too flat.

Outside, the river flowed beside us, dark and fast. I'd heard stories of buses and jeeps disappearing into its depths, of landslides swallowing whole villages. The hills and water had seen so much loss, it was as if they carried the memory of grief in their bones.

Death hovered nearby. Closer than I wanted to admit.

As we neared Malekhu—famous for its fish—Laxman *dai* smiled and mentioned how easy we were together on the road. He shared stories of his time with the Pokhara Commercial Federation and how he loved helping others.

I nodded, telling him I couldn't stand to see people in pain.

Then he said something that stuck with me. "If my mother-in-law hadn't passed, we wouldn't be sharing this ride."

I watched the rushing Trishuli River. His words echoed in my mind, but I wasn't sure how to respond. Not everything could be explained.

Laxman *dai* smiled, pleased with my response. By then, we had arrived at Nagdhunga, the gateway to Kathmandu. My father-in-law had risen and was looking out the window. From the dizzying heights of Thankot hills, we could see a trail of vehicles winding below us, like a serpent. The road still sent chills down my spine, a remnant of past fears.

I turned toward Laxman *dai*, reassuring him, "We'll be at my house in a few minutes," as I continued to gaze out at the view.

It was 10:30 in the morning by the time we reached Kalanki, which was always busy due to the buses and trucks that frequented the Kathmandu valley. It would take us some time to get through Kalanki. We followed the ring road via Balkhu and Satdobato and took an exit at Balkumari chowk. When we reached my house, an hour had passed.

My parents had already made food since I had informed them we were coming. We didn't talk much. We were grieving and my father-in-law was in pain as well. We ate dinner, me without salt. My father-in-law had lost his appetite, so he didn't eat more than a morsel of the rice and a little bit of green vegetable curry. He sipped a bit of lentil soup. That day we rested at home, chatted with my parents, and decided to go see a doctor the next day.

Chapter Five

Smoke and Smile's Longevity

December 3, 2019

We had planned to see Dr. Sashi, a gastro specialist, at his private clinic at a teaching hospital in nearby Maharajganj. The doctors in Pokhara had also advised my father-in-law to go see him.

Kathmandu's weather was typically colder than in Pokhara, and winter had arrived.

My *sasuraba* was awake by six o'clock.

It didn't take long for me to see; however, he was in a lot of pain.

A few minutes later, my parents and Laxman *dai* got up and came to the living room.

"You can go see the doctor after eating some breakfast," my mother said, starting toward the kitchen upstairs.

"Don't trouble yourself, *Samdhini jyu*. I don't have any appetite right now. It is too early. We would rather find something on the way. Kathmandu has a great deal of traffic, so we should leave early," my father-in-law said.

"If so, I will make black tea. At least have a drink before you go," my mother insisted.

While sitting in the living room and talking about my father-in-law's sickness and pain, my mother brought a few cups of steaming liquid on *Kisti*, a square-shaped serving plate.

"We both have diabetes," my mother said.

She lifted a separate sugar-free teacup and handed it to my father-in-law. My father, Laxman *dai* and I took a cup from the serving plate as she offered it to each of us.

"The tea is excellent, *Samdhini jyu*," my father-in-law said while sipping. "What did you put in it?"

"Cardamom, black pepper, cloves, and bay leaves."

"Oh! You made it taste so delicious. I think this will heal my ailment."

"*Samdhi saheb,* your appreciation makes me happy. Thank you," my mother said with a smile. "I don't know what the doctor will say about your pain. Please ask him for details."

"Hope everything will be fine," he said, trying to get up.

My father-in-law, Laxman *dai* and I left the house and got into Laxman *dai's* car, which had been a huge help in getting us from one place to another. He started the engine and warmed it up a little bit before we left. On the road, the traffic had already gotten denser with school buses, micro buses, trucks, and trippers. Grocery store shutters were open, and vegetable vendors had already spread their goods out on the footpath.

As we arrived at Ratnapark, my *sasuraba* smiled at me and pointed to where street vendors were selling their items.

"This is where I used to sell ready-made clothes on the footpath, standing and talking to customers and passersby. At that time, your wife—my daughter Kripa—was just born."

"I never knew that. Then it must have been around 1987 or '88."

"That's right. I didn't see many vehicles on the road, nor were there tall buildings like these," he said, looking outside the window and pointing to them. "Your mother-in-law and I worked hard back then. But now there are numerous roads and gullies. It's confusing to me." He became nostalgic and emotional. I did the math and figured out that it was his story from thirty years ago.

"How many times did you visit Kathmandu after that?"

"Once or twice, I don't remember, but it was a long time ago."

Laxman *dai* was driving. The amount of traffic increased. Horns honked and vehicles took over the road. The pedestrians increased, too, crossing by the skybridge and zebra crossings.

We arrived at Dr. Shashi's private clinic at eight thirty in the morning and signed our names on the patient list. After we got there, we found out patients wouldn't be seen for more than six hours. We went home for lunch.

On the way, Kripa called me to get an update on her father.

After we ate, we returned to the clinic—this time battling thick traffic that stretched the drive to more than an hour. Dr. Shashi was due at three o'clock, but he arrived thirty minutes late.

Four patients were ahead of us, and it was nearly five o'clock by the time we stepped inside. I had the backpack slung over my shoulder, heavy with X-rays, CT scans, and every report I could gather—proof of everything we didn't yet understand.

Dr. Shashi's office was a well-organized room adorned with certifications and informative posters. A tidy desk with a computer and essential medical instruments occupied one side, while shelves holding categorized reference books lined the walls. The room had ample natural light, creating a calming atmosphere, and was furnished with comfortable chairs for patients and their companions.

Although he had a youthful appearance—a skinny fellow with a big smile—he was probably over sixty years of age. For twenty years, he had served as a university professor and helped train many doctors.

With this in mind, I asked if he knew Dr. Puspamani Kharal. He said, "Of course! He was my student."

Dr. Kharal had lived with me in America for three months. He was there to volunteer at Boca Regional Hospital in Boca Raton, Florida. An MD in Medical Science and a general family practitioner, Dr. Kharal resided in Kathmandu and worked at his own clinic after his residencies at various hospitals in Nepal.

Dr. Shashi asked general questions, the kind every doctor asks when a patient visits them.

I explained everything to him—my father-in-law's ailment, his stomach pain, his ulcer from twenty years ago. As I talked, he scribbled on the prescription report paper and asked the patient to lie down on the bed in the room.

"Can you please pull your shirt above your belly?" Dr. Shashi asked, and my father-in-law followed his instructions accordingly. The big scar from his ulcer surgery loomed large, as if fresh and new.

"Is this the scar from your previous surgery?"

"Does it hurt? Here? Here?"

"Ouch! Ouch!" My father-in-law shrieked in pain every time the doctor pressed on his abdomen.

"Okay, now you can get up," the physician said, taking off the gloves and washing his hands at the sink nearby.

My father-in-law sat in a chair. The doctor lifted the CT scan results and placed them on the film viewer, inspecting them carefully. He said, "I want you to do another CT scan. I think you did this in Pokhara. Sometimes the machine can make a mistake, so let's do another one somewhere I recommend. That way I can be one hundred percent confident about your diagnosis. Only then can I give you my recommendations."

When an experienced specialist asked for more scans, there was no point in arguing. Our goal was to cure my father-in-law's suffering and get back home as soon as possible. That was the hope. That was the wish.

"One more thing, Doctor Shashi. His pain is intolerable. Isn't there any medicine that could help him feel better for the time being?" I asked.

"How can I prescribe you the right medicine without being sure what kind of affliction it is?" Dr. Shashi said. "Go do the CT scan at this location. The name of it is Imaging CT Scan. This is on Darbar Marg near the Yak and Yeti hotel. It's open twenty-four hours. Please return with the report."

At times I wondered why he didn't offer medication since the patient was suffering and needed his pain managed.

"Sure," we said and left his office.

As soon as we stepped outside, Dr. Shashi called me, saying, "Please come back in alone. I will tell you about some medicine." I told Laxman *dai* and my father-in-law to wait for me in the lobby and went back to Dr. Shashi's room.

He did not tell me about any medication, but there was a reason for calling me back in.

"You need to understand that your father-in-law's disease is advanced. Reviewing the CT scan from Pokhara, it appears he has a tumor in his pancreas, so I want to make sure the CT scan is right," Dr. Shashi said, holding up the CT scan for me to see. "Did he ever drink alcohol to excess?"

How could he directly say the cause of cancer could be only alcohol? I couldn't wrap my head around what he was saying. My hands and feet trembled. *How would his daughters react if they heard this?*

"Yes, Dr. Saap, he did drink a lot before, but he quit. He has not had any alcohol for the last three years, since he developed diabetes and started taking insulin."

In all honesty, my father-in-law drank quite a bit of alcohol previously, especially when he worked in his own restaurant and traveled back and forth from India to Nepal. He often drank with his friends. "This alcohol gave me confidence and courage, *Jwaisaap*, so I managed to build this three-story house in the heart of the Sisuwa chowk here," he used to tell me with pride, almost bragging about his heavy alcohol use.

"That's the reason he is suffering now. Your father-in-law damaged his system a long time ago. Anyway, please bring me the CT scan report tomorrow, and we will go from there. Don't let your father-in-law know about this now," Dr. Shashi advised.

I nodded in agreement. I was already stressed out and sweating.

"Doctor, my mother-in-law was bringing him to Kathmandu for treatment three days ago, but she fell on the road and died. The doctor said it was a heart attack. Her daughters are now in mourning, and so I am taking my *sasuraba* to see you. If he were healthy and hearty, the daughters could at least have some hope for life," I said.

Listening to me speak, Dr. Shashi remained quiet and speechless, gazing first at the ceiling blankly, and then back to me.

"Please do not stress yourself right now," he replied. "First, I will read the report, and then I will tell you." His words sounded comforting to me, but the doctor's explanation had already started to haunt me.

"Sure," I said as I left the room.

My father-in-law and Laxman *dai* were sitting outside in the lobby waiting for me. Laxman *dai* examined my face, suspecting why the doctor called me in separately. My father-in-law was staring into the distance as if fighting the stomach pain.

"Let's go to the Imaging Center and get the scan right away," I said. It was half past five in the evening in the winter, and the days were getting shorter. The rush hour congestion was heavy. People were finishing their work and heading home or somewhere else for shopping or other errands. The sun was about to set. Sunrays the color of turmeric gave Kathmandu a golden hue. Dust continued to rise and flicker like gold flecks, reminding me of a poem by Maya Angelou:

...Just like moons and like suns,
With the certainty of tides,
Just like hopes Springing high,
Still, I'll rise...
— from "Still I Rise" by Maya Angelou

The traffic was suffocating—cars, taxies, thronging motorcycles. I felt myself gasping for air, not because of the traffic, but because of what Dr. Shashi had said.

"At least we have a car, right, brother?" Laxman *dai* said with pride, breaking into the stream of my silent thoughts.

"You are right, *dai*," I said, trying to offer my praise. "If we didn't have your car, how could we manage to go back and forth and do all these things?"

I was more worried about my father-in-law's report and the potential results. I silently kept him in my prayers. I had no one to share this with, not even Kripa. I pressed the feeling down within myself, but I felt like it would explode out of me. I had no alternative but to control my emotions and stay optimistic.

When we were minutes from the Imaging Center, Kripa called me. "Where are you?"

"We are going to the center for your father's CT scan."

"We had the CT scan report from Pokhara," she said.

"The doctor wants to do another one. Just to be certain."

"Why do these doctors give us trouble?" Kripa asked, her voice tired and concerned and filled with empathy.

Attempting to change the subject, I asked, "How are you? Hope you are eating enough even if it is not salty."

"Yes, I am, but my blood pressure has dropped. I am feeling jittery."

"Yes, it is because you have not eaten salty food for some days. If you get sick what will happen to our one-year-old daughter? I think you should talk to the priest to see if you need to eat normal for our daughter. How is Krisha doing? Is she eating too?"

"Sure, I will talk to the priest. Yes, Krisha is fine. Don't worry. *Fupudidi* is looking after her," she said.

"You don't have to worry about your father. I am here with him."

We arrived at the Imaging Center, but there was no place to park. In America, there had to be designated parking areas at any medical building, but in Nepal we usually didn't have that luxury. Perhaps it was because many people in Nepal couldn't afford cars.

"I will drop you off here and find a place to park the car. Then I'll come back," Laxman *dai* said.

We got out of the car. I supported my father-in-law, holding his hand, and we both entered the building. Telling my father-in-law to sit in the chair nearby, I went to the reception to ask for a CT scan.

"Do you have the patient's blood and urine test reports?" asked a young girl at the reception desk.

Some said that a CT scan didn't require a urine test, only blood work to check kidney function. However, we had to follow their suggestions. She was in her early twenties. Dressed in blue kurta and suruwal, her hair was pinned up in a bun. Light skinned and pretty, she spoke like she was tired of talking to patients and their attendants. *We shouldn't judge someone's beauty based on their outward appearance.* She'd lost her ability to smile. There wasn't an ounce of customer service in her attitude.

"I have all the reports here," I said.

I took them from my backpack and handed them over to her.

"I don't see your urine test report here," she said, flipping through the papers. "You'll have to do that one." Her tone was rude.

"There it is," I said, pointing to the one she was missing.

"This report is from more than a week ago. The report must be done within a week," she said callously. The reports were from when he had seen the doctors in Pokhara.

How sweet and beautiful that same statement would sound if she had spoken softly and in a friendly or professional manner. My perception and understanding of customer service and professionalism had changed significantly when I had the opportunity to visit America.

"Where would I do the test?" I asked, frustrated. I was already stressed out knowing the doctor's prediction about my father-in-law's pancreatic tumor. On top of that, there were a million things to be done before a CT scan. So much stress. So much confusion. *Shit!*

"We have labs around everywhere," she said while tapping the keyboard on the computer in front of her. "You can go to Bagbazzar." I took a long breath and let it go, trying to calm the unease rising in me. Telling my father-in-law to continue sitting for a while, I went outside. Laxman *dai* had arrived after parking his car elsewhere.

"*Dai*, we have to bring in a urine test report before doing the CT scan. It would be ideal if we could do it today. The receptionist says there are many labs in Bagbazzar where we can do his test," I said.

Since yesterday, his morning walk involved more running around here and there with me for my father-in-law's treatment. His belly appeared shrunken a bit from before. All that rushing around might have helped him lose his belly fat more than his morning walk.

"My father-in-law's condition is serious, *dai*," I continued since I couldn't keep the secret. As soon as I shared this with him, I felt relieved. "Dr. Shashi believes he has a tumor in his pancreas. I hope this CT scan will show something different."

I studied Laxman *dai's* eyes. The suspicion I had seen earlier now confirmed.

"Really?" He acted as if he were surprised. "What can we do? Let's wait for the second report. Let me pick you up, and we can go to Bagbazzar for the urine test." With the key in his hand, he went to get the car.

He returned with the car, and I helped my father-in-law into the back seat. I climbed in front, and we headed toward Bagbazzar for the test.

The sun had already dipped below the horizon. Headlights cut through the dusk, sharp and glittering, but the roads were jammed with motorcycles and honking horns.

We crawled past Darbar Marga and turned near Ratnapark, scanning for a lab. When we finally spotted one tucked along a one-way street, I jumped out and rushed to the reception desk.

"We are about to close. You'll have to return tomorrow," one of the workers said as if he were ready to head home as soon as possible.

"Oh, really? What time do you close?" I asked.

"Seven."

My watch confirmed it was a quarter to seven.

"There are still fifteen minutes before you close, sir. Can you please do the urine test? It is an emergency. Please do this for us."

They accepted my plea. They took both urine and blood from my father-in-law's arm and told us to wait. Within fifteen minutes, the reports came in.

"You see, I am fine. All the reports are fine. These doctors do nothing. They only want to milk money," my father-in-law muttered. He sounded satisfied, as if there was nothing wrong with him, all the while pressing on his belly with one hand to assuage the pain. "Why can't they find the real cause of my stomach pain, my disease?"

"Perhaps we will know after the CT scan, *Buwa*," I said, getting back in the car again, but fear was building inside me. I contemplated the matter silently, fairly sure my father-in-law had a serious disease.

We were extremely tired from rushing around the entire day. We went back to the Imaging Center with the report in our hands. At least the Imaging Center was open twenty-four hours. I placed all the reports in front of the receptionist. I realized my father-in-law wouldn't have been able to get the CT scan if his urine test had shown any issues. I gave her 12,000 Nepali rupees for the CT scan charge and waited for our turn, which took almost two hours. In the meantime, they had given him a liter bottle of water to drink.

"Yes, it takes time. Please finish drinking this bottle of water. It contains medicine to ready you for the CT scan. We'll be able to see things clearly in the report," the receptionist said. "Try not to pee until the CT scan."

I left my father-in-law and Laxman *dai* in the reception area and stepped outside to relieve my stress. When I was stressed and exhausted, I usually smoked a cigarette. A pan pasal betelnut stall was nearby, facing toward the Royal Palace. I purchased a Surya cigarette and lit it.

What the fuck. This life was nothing—so fragile. You never knew when your own life would run its course. You don't know what sickness or disease you might be carrying.

I sucked on the cigarette, drawing in the smoke—its burn mixing with the exhaust from passing vehicles, all of it hanging thick in the air.

Lights from the street and glittering billboard advertisements illuminated the former royal palace. On the first of June 2001, all five members of the royal family had been assassinated. The royal massacre. In a place with such high security, death had entered and caused devastation. *Who could predict their own time to die?*

I ruminated over these thoughts as I stared at the royal palace and exhaled smoke that rose into the night sky. *Life.*

I couldn't bring myself to say it—not to Kripa, not while she mourned her mother. If it was cancer, the news would break her.

And Buwa—what if it drained his strength just to know?

My parents... what could they do with the truth, except carry it?

So, I held it. The weight of it. Quietly.

The palace now had been converted into a museum. The monarchy had collapsed, and the country had become a democratic republic. But the country's problems were the same as before. I took a final drag of the cigarette and tossed it. I bought two Happy Dents gums to prevent bad breath and put them into my mouth. I returned to where my father-in-law and Laxman *dai* were waiting for the CT scan.

"Did you finish drinking the bottle of water?" I asked. The bottle of water included some sort of medicine mixed with water for the CT scan.

"Almost," he answered.

He was in pain—I could tell from his face—but he acted hopeful about getting treatment. He finished the water in a few gulps, and his turn came right away. After half an hour, the CT scan was over.

"Please come tomorrow to get your report," said the receptionist in a menacing tone, looking more exasperated than ever.

I agreed because there was no rush; we couldn't see Dr. Shashi any earlier than tomorrow. We decided to go to the Imaging Center first, get the report, then go see the doctor.

It was nine in the evening and the traffic on the road was thinning.

"At least we won't be in a traffic jam since it's late," I said, exhaling the worry I hadn't realized I'd been holding. "We managed to do a lot today. Now we must wait for the report tomorrow. Let's see."

"Indeed. It is all because we had a car," Laxman *dai* added, proud of himself and his car. He was right, of course, but his frequent boasts about himself and his car were becoming tiresome.

Still, I backed him up, saying, "That's true *dai*. If we didn't have your car, we wouldn't be able to do all those things."

It was late evening when we got home to Tikathali. My parents had made dinner and were waiting for us. My mother served us food—lentil soup, rice, green vegetables. I briefly reported what we did during the day. My father-in-law was still pressing his belly with his hands and in extreme pain. He sat to eat but could not swallow more than a morsel. He sipped a little bit of lentil soup. We worried about him.

We all went to bed. I called my beautiful wife Kripa and asked about her and Krisha before I fell asleep.

"We will know only after we show the report to the doctor tomorrow," I said to Kripa, trying to sound reassuring. "Good night."

I ached for them. Krisha's birthday, the reason for my visit to Nepal, was approaching rapidly. It seemed like a distant hope amidst all the unfortunate events that had occurred. Frustrated, I whispered to myself, "I won't be able to celebrate my child's first birthday."

Chapter Six

American Dream's Flight

December 4, 2019

I couldn't help thinking morbid thoughts as I reflected on my *sasuma's* death and s*asuraba's* illness. Naturally, people want to avoid the subject, but it couldn't be avoided forever. Plato, in his philosophical dialogue titled *Phaedo*, wisely wrote those preparing for death won't be troubled by it. People were troubled by sickness and death only when they were not prepared for it. Thus, perhaps it was good to remind oneself about sickness and death. Lailah Gifty Akita in his book *Pearls of Wisdom: Great Mind* writes, "We must be conscious of this; one day, the life we have, will be gone."

Like the day before, my father-in-law was already awake by six o'clock, sitting in the living room with his hands resting on his stomach, lips pursed and wincing. Our appointment with Dr. Shashi wasn't until three o'clock, but we needed to pick up the CT scan report from the Imaging Center beforehand. Rushing wouldn't make the day go any faster.

"*Buwa*, you woke up early today, too. I see you didn't sleep well," I said, clearing my throat. My voice felt gravelly, perhaps because yesterday was spent talking with people and breathing in a lot of dust on the roads of Kathmandu.

"It's been like this for a while, *Jwaisaap*," he said, his eyes tired and dim. "I would rather the pleasure of dying early than bearing this pain and enduring sleepless nights."

It had been three months since he'd had a full night's sleep. I remembered what he had once said: "Our days are almost over now, *Jwaisaap*. Your days and your children's days are coming. You should celebrate them." I turned his words over in my mind.

Laxman *dai* also joined us in the living room, wiping his eyes and trying to refresh himself. "Good morning!"

"Good morning, *dai*," I said, trying to turn the TV on using the remote on the tea table. "Did you get enough sleep?"

"I slept well, *Jwaisaap*. Perhaps I was tired from yesterday. As soon as I lay down on the bed, I fell asleep. And came in here as soon as I woke up," he said, as he sat on the couch.

My mother went upstairs to make tea. The rest of us watched the morning news on the TV hanging on the wall.

In the news, the U.S. Government's Millenium Challenge Corporation (MCC) remained a hot topic, as the Standing Committee members of the ruling Nepal Communist Party claimed the MCC was a part of Washington's Indo-Pacific Strategy.

After a minute or two, my mother brought in cups of tea, including one sugar-free.

"What time is your meeting with the doctor today?" my father asked, sipping the tea. His slurping echoed in the living room.

This reminded me of a previous incident involving slurping. After my U.S. roommate told me "You have no manners" when I unknowingly slurped my tea, I became aware of this difference in cultural etiquette. From that point on, I made a conscious effort to drink without creating any noise. However, during this adjustment period, I experienced instances where hot tea would scald my tongue until I gradually grew accustomed to the temperature.

"Today we have to get the CT scan report first and meet with the doctor at three o'clock, so we will eat some lunch before we leave," I said, turning down the volume on the TV.

"I think the report should come out fine. Sometimes gastritis also causes strong pain. Most Nepali people have gastritis that causes all kinds of sickness. Again, you have diabetes, too, so ..." my father said, offering his own diagnosis as he shared his focus between me and his *Samdhi*, my father-in-law.

My *sasuraba* stretched his body, trying to assuage his pain.

"I'm not sure what it is," he said. "The doctors don't know what is happening inside me. *Samdhi Saap*, how many doctors have I seen now? One doctor gives me one type of medicine and another doctor gives me another type of medicine. At times I think they are all charlatans." He vented frustration at his unbearable pain.

"You are right, *Samdhi Saap*. If you don't take the medicine the doctor has recommended, you might feel worse. If you do take it, it could cause another side effect," my father said over each sip. My father was loud when he spoke.

Laxman *dai* was playing with the phone, scrolling through his Facebook newsfeed while he murmured in agreement: "Yes, yes."

We had already finished our tea, and time crawled by slowly. My mother made lunch on *jharke thals*, copper plates used to serve special guests out of hospitality. She called us to come to the kitchen upstairs. The food was laid out on the dining room table. We sat down to eat. My father-in-law asked for most of the meal to be removed from his plate since he wouldn't be able to eat it.

"Oh, *Samdhi Saap*, you don't eat any food at all. How can you be strong?" my father said, taking the rice away and leaving a little bit on the plate. "Are you still thinking about your wife? She is gone. She cannot come back. Nothing is under our control. You must take care of yourself. You must be brave and strong for your daughters and grandchildren. You must think about your health. When you're strong, only then can you do everything. Try to force yourself to eat more and fight this disease."

"You are right, *Samdhi Saap*. I want to eat more, but I don't have any appetite at all. I cannot eat. I have tried. I was not this type of person before. I always ate a lot, much more than I should. I could eat anything and digest anything. Since I became sick, especially for the last three months, I haven't been able to eat much," my father-in-law responded with difficulty, trying to eat a little bit from the plate.

"I hear you," my mother added, arranging the pots and pans filled with food and clinking the cutlery. "Please get good consultations from the doctor today, and get well soon."

We all got up after lunch. It was almost eleven o'clock.

"Perhaps we should go now because we also have to get the CT scan report on the way. Again, there is a lot of traffic in the Kathmandu Valley," Laxman *dai* proposed after he finished scraping his plate clean.

"Sounds good to me," I said, washing my hands and mouth after the meal.

We left the house, got my *sasuraba* into the car, and drove to the imaging center. There was heavy traffic on the way. The dust and pollution were dense, an issue Kathmanduites had to cope with every day. As we passed Koteswor next to the airport, planes were taking off and landing right above us—Buddha Air, Yeti Airlines, Turkish Airlines, Qatar Airways. The hills in the distance appeared to be caked with dust. Once visible from the city, the closest mountain to Kathmandu, Jugal, had disappeared into the haze. We reached the imaging center via Putali Sadak.

"Is our report available?" I asked at reception, where I found a different receptionist, much friendlier than the one I spoke to the day before.

"Can you please tell me the name of the patient?" she asked, clicking the mouse and looking at the computer screen in front of her.

"Resham Lal Bhandari."

The report was ready. She took an envelope from her desk and printed the report, put it into the envelope, and handed it over to me.

"Thank you."

I couldn't wait. I sent up a quick prayer and slid the report from the envelope. My eyes landed on the bottom—something underlined.

Androgenic Cancer.

The word punched through me. My heart started to race.

I stared at the page, willing my face to stay still, my hands slick with sweat. I didn't want them to see. Not yet.

"How is the report, *Jwaisaap*?" Laxman *dai* asked while he drove. He gave me a quick glance and cleared his throat.

I couldn't tell him what I saw on the report because my father-in-law was in the back seat. I tried to control my heartbeat.

"I'm not able to understand it, *dai*, by looking at the report. I think we should wait to see what the doctor has to say."

Within minutes, we arrived at Metro Polyclinic—two hours early for our appointment. On the top floor, we found a small café and decided to wait there over tea.

We sat at a plastic table with mismatched chairs and ordered three cups. My father-in-law asked for *belleka roti* with yogurt—his favorite—and I was glad to get it for him. The air was crisp, and the sun had slipped behind a bank of gray clouds.

From our table, I could see the American Embassy across the road. Guards stood at attention, eyes scanning the line of people waiting outside. Probably there for visa interviews. The sight pulled me back to 2008, when I stood in that same line, heart pounding, filled with hope and uncertainty, clutching my future in a folder.

Many of those in line were denied a visa and had returned with their eyes full of tears. I had also cried, but they were tears of joy when I was granted a visa. It had felt like a dream when I received it. That was twelve years ago—twelve years since I had started living in the United States—and yet the line in front of the embassy was longer than ever.

The desire to leave hadn't faded. If anything, it had grown. In Nepal, getting an American visa was still considered a status symbol, a kind of victory. I couldn't help but wonder: *when would we begin to believe that our dreams could be realized here, at home? When would staying feel like enough?*

"*Jwai*, where did you get lost?" Laxman *dai* asked with a smile, startling me, breaking the flow of my thoughts. "Your tea is almost cold. Drink it up."

I felt like someone had jostled me from behind or jammed on the breaks in a vehicle hurtling at high speeds—that vehicle was my nostalgia. I lifted the cup up and found that my tea was already cold. I quaffed it. The vehicles were racing by on the road below. A glance at my watch confirmed it was half past two. Only a half hour left now. We were informed that the doctor had arrived in his office.

"The doctor came on time today," I said to myself jokingly as I carried the report into his office.

"Namaste, Doctor Saap!"

"Where is your patient?" the doctor asked, returning my greetings and reaching out to me for the report.

"He is outside."

Dr. Shashi studied the report I handed him and said, "Now it is sure. What I told you yesterday is now confirmed. He has a tumor in the pancreas. Your father-in-law has cancer. He damaged it a long time ago, and treatment is impossible now, I think."

While the doctor was explaining the diagnosis, my heart throbbed. I could hear it thundering in my ears, as if it was trying to break free. Everything felt dark. I sought comfort in the face of Laxman dai, but all I saw there was confusion — a mirrored reflection of my own helplessness. My hands were sweating. I pondered how to break the news to my wife and her sister, who still mourned the recent loss of their mother. Those thoughts were painful, but there was no other alternative but to be optimistic.

Oh, dear God, why do you engage in such games? Why do you act so unjustly? What wrong was committed by the daughters to deserve this additional misery you're inflicting upon them? How will they find the strength to cope with the news of their father's cancer while grieving the loss of their mother? How can I remain calm and maintain a positive outlook, believing that everything happens for a reason?

"Please, don't let the patient know about this now. If possible, show this report to another doctor here at the clinic. His name is Dr. Bikalp. He's a specialist in this type of disease. He usually arrives around four in the afternoon, so get some advice from him," Dr. Shashi said, handing the report back to me.

Panic was already clawing at my chest, and anxiety was tightening its noose. I had no alternative but to control myself because I had to take care of Kripa and my daughter. As Kripa's husband, I found myself immersed in her situation, as her story had intertwined with my own. Although I naturally tend to be an emotional person, the weight of responsibility resting upon my shoulders compelled me to embody bravery and strength.

"Sure, Dr. Saap," I said with confidence, although my voice was shaking.

"Don't stress out. Whatever must happen will happen," Dr. Shashi said, trying to comfort me.

As we left the doctor's office I said to Laxman *dai*, "*Dai*, let's not tell anyone about this. Let's keep this a secret. We shouldn't tell this to Kripa and Suman. We should just say that the doctor has given medicine, and he will be okay."

"Of course, we should not let them know about it right now," Laxman *dai* said, trying to be supportive. My father-in-law was pressing his belly with his hands and sitting in the lobby area waiting for us and the report. One could see the fire of pain flaring up in his face.

"*Buwa*, let's meet another doctor, Dr. Bikalp. We've been referred to him. He is an expert in the type of disease that you have," I said, gesturing for him to get up. "That is what Dr. Shashi recommended."

"Which doctor, again?" he asked, trying to stand on his shaky legs, but he was very listless. "Why do these doctors give me a hard time?"

He stretched his body while pressing his mouth tight, perhaps to assuage his unbearable pain.

"What is the pain like right now, on a scale of one to ten?" I asked. "Keep in mind, ten represents the highest level of pain."

"Isn't there a level one hundred?" he responded, making clear the intensity of the pain he endured.

I purchased a ticket for a second appointment and we waited for Dr. Bikalp, who didn't arrive until five in the afternoon. The man was in his late forties, quiet and almost callous. As soon as he arrived, we showed him all the reports and discussed Dr. Sashi's recommendation. He took some time to go through the report and asked us about the patient's medical history.

"Did you use to drink alcohol, *Buwa*?" Dr. Bikalp asked my father-in-law.

He pressed around the stomach with his gloved hands. I found his voice kind, but I was terrified: *What if the doctor told my father-in-law he had cancer?*

He didn't, and a wave of relief washed over me.

"Yes, a few years back."

"How much?"

"I might have drunk until it was enough for me. Now it has been three years since I quit."

"You seem to have made a mistake a long time ago and jeopardized your health," the doctor said. "Let's do one thing. Please see me tomorrow at nine o'clock at the teaching hospital."

The sun was down by then.

"Yes, Dr. Saap," we said. We returned home to Tikathali. On the way back home, Kripa had called me twice, but I didn't answer because I didn't know what to say if she asked me about the doctor's diagnosis regarding her father's CT scan.

"It's been almost three days, and Kripa hasn't called," my father-in-law complained. He remembered his daughters.

"She has been calling me, *Buwa*," I said, trying to comfort him.

"Yes, but 'you' is not 'me.' I also have a phone in my pocket," he shot back right away. I understood his feelings toward his daughter.

I secretly texted Kripa: "Please call your father on his phone. He is disappointed in you, his feelings are hurt because you haven't called him."

Kripa called him right away. My father-in-law's face brightened with joy when he answered the phone. For a moment he forgot his pain.

Who else would be left among the most cherished individuals in his life after the loss of his wife? Only Kripa and Suman. I found myself there solely because of Kripa. Without her, I would be devoid of purpose.

I called Kripa back before I went to sleep that night.

"Why didn't you answer my call when I called you twice?" Kripa complained on the phone, her voice sad.

"I was with the doctors and couldn't answer," I said, tossing and turning on the bed. I lied to her a bit.

"What did the doctor say?" she asked with hope.

"What could he say? Nothing. Not to worry too much. But the doctor has called us to see him at the teaching hospital tomorrow," I said, hiding under the blanket in bed. "I am missing Krisha. How is she doing? I want to see her and speak."

"She has already fallen asleep. Let's talk tomorrow. I have a headache too. I want to sleep," Kripa said, sounding tired.

"Okay, good night, baby. Sleep well," I said despite my racing thoughts.

Chapter Seven

Truth's Pain and Illusion's Joy

December 5, 2019

It was half past seven by the time we got to the car. We reached the hospital a half hour later, an hour before the scheduled appointment. Living in America had made me acutely aware of the significance of time. Unlike in Nepal, where events and programs often began half an hour or even an hour late, punctuality was deeply ingrained in American culture. This stark contrast gave rise to the infamous notion of "Nepali time." Life in America had taught me many lessons—especially about the value of time and the importance of a strong work ethic.

We were called to the surgical ward in the hospital. All the medical reports were in my backpack. "Where is Dr. Bikalp?" I asked a young man in a white jacket. "We have a meeting with him at nine o'clock"

"It's not nine o'clock yet. Why have you come so early? He is in a meeting," the man in the white jacket said abruptly without looking at me. He was staring at the reception area where nurses were collecting the patients' documents, as if he didn't want to talk to anyone. He sounded rude. Later, I learned he was Dr. Bikalp's assistant and was doing an internship there, carrying the patients' medical reports and following the doctor's orders.

"Yes, we came early because we thought the sooner we came, the earlier we could meet the doctor," I said, trying to sound kind and logical, my hand swatting at a fly that passed by my nose.

"Come later," he said with the same tone, but this time he made eye contact. He had tiny eyes and tight lips.

"Your good name, please?" I asked. He ignored my question and acted like he preferred not to tell me his name. He asked a lady at reception to search for the documents for a patient he named. "I will give you a call before I return if you give me your phone number."

Finally, he let me know his name was Dipesh. His forehead puckered and eyes glared angrily as he said it. He gave me his phone number and took mine, saying, "When the doctor comes out from the meeting, I will give you a call. No need to call me." Then he left.

When I still hadn't heard from him at half past nine, I tried giving him a call.

"Hasn't Dr. Bikalp come out from the meeting? It's half past nine now," I said.

"He already came out and entered the surgical ward for the patient's operation. You can go home if you want to. I will call you later," he uttered the words in a stern and uncaring tone, conveying a sense of indifference.

We didn't go home. We had to speak with Dr. Bikalp and get answers.

I hovered outside the Operation Theatre, checking in with staff, hoping to catch the doctor the moment he stepped out. I couldn't trust Dipesh to follow through.

My father-in-law and Laxman *dai* sat quietly on the ground near the entrance, huddled in the morning sun for warmth. The chill clung to everything.

I paced the hall and ran into Dipesh again.

"Is Dr. Bikalp out of the OT now?" I asked.

"I told you—I'll call," he snapped, not looking up from his file.

I bit my tongue and walked away. It was nearly noon. We still hadn't eaten, and I was starting to shake from more than the cold.

My *sasuraba* pleaded with a heavy heart in his eyes. "I want to go back to Pokhara. My heart is fluttering. My daughters are in mourning. I wonder what my poor kids might be doing. If I was there, I could at least give them advice and direction. I'm starting to feel suffocated and sicker than ever." His voice sounded helpless and desperate.

People were everywhere—sitting on the ground, leaning on crutches, crowded in front of the OPD ticket counter. Some waited in silence, eyes hollow with pain. Others jostled and shouted, trying to be heard.

It felt like all of Nepal had come here to be treated. The noise, the motion, the weight of so much suffering—I couldn't imagine how anyone stayed well in a place like this.

The contrast with American hospitals was stark. There, everything was ordered, quiet, private. Here, illness was something shared, out in the open.

"*Buwa*, don't get stressed out. Your daughters are doing what they are supposed to do. Your Jaya *jwai* is there. The sooner we address your illness, the earlier you can go home. We have come here to see the doctor for your treatment. Let's see what Dr. Bikalp has to say," I said, holding my *sasuraba's* hand and caressing it.

Dipesh called. "Where are you now? Dr. Bikalp is right here. Come fast."

A while ago, he said that we could go home, and now he demanded that we "come fast." The whole thing made me angry. I was hungry and tired and stressed out, but my anger would not fix the situation, so we rushed to the meeting without exchanging a word.

"Please bring *Buwa* with you slowly, I will run and see the doctor first before he disappears again," I said to Laxman *dai*. A throng of people were moving up and down on the stairs, and I pushed my way through them at a dead run. The surgical ward was on the third floor. By the time I got there, I was panting.

"Dr. Saap, *namaskar*!" I called out, breathing fast.

"Where is your patient?" he said without returning my greetings.

"He is coming slowly." There was no lift for the patients to get to the upper floors.

Dr. Bikalp returned to Dipesh, his expression focused. "Please take them downstairs for the FNA tests. I want to see the patient's report," he instructed, then turned to me. "After you get the report, please come and see me." Confusion washed over me; I had no idea what an FNA test entailed.

"Sure, Dr. *Saap*," I replied, trying to sound composed.

We made our way back to Room 6 on the first floor. My father-in-law had climbed the stairs, and now he had to go back down. Each step was a struggle. I stayed close behind him, afraid he might fall.

I searched "FNA test" on my phone, needing to understand. *Needle biopsy*, the screen said. Reading it made my stomach twist. It felt like we were inching closer to the word we hadn't said out loud yet.

After what felt like an eternity, my father-in-law's name was called.

A nurse handed me a list of medications and supplies. Without meeting my eyes, she flipped the paper toward me.

"You'll need to buy these."

I left him with Laxman *dai* and rushed to the pharmacy. The total came to forty dollars—an amount that hit hard in a place where even breathing felt heavy. I shoved the receipt into my pocket and hurried back, my hands trembling as I passed the bag to the waiting nurse.

A knot had already formed in my stomach. Something didn't feel right.

Suddenly, a sharp scream tore through the hallway.

"I am dying!"

It was my *sasuraba*.

I froze. His voice—so raw, so full of pain—cut straight through me. My heart pounded. I gripped the chair beside me to keep from rushing in. I couldn't see what was happening, but I didn't need to. The sound was enough.

I felt useless. Like I'd failed him already.

Within fifteen minutes, the procedure was done. The doctors finished inserting the needle into his belly and patched up the wound with clinical efficiency, but the sound of my *sasuraba's* cries lingered in the air, a haunting reminder of the emotional toll this journey was exacting on all of us

My *sasuraba* came out with his hands clenching his belly. "They nearly killed me. It is very painful." He continued moaning in pain. There was a bed for him to rest a while. The doctor had taken the cells from his pancreas. Those cells would now need to go to the lab for examination. The nurse handed me the tube and said, "Take it to the second floor, Room 6, and leave it there."

I turned to *Sasuraba* and Laxman *dai* and said, "Please stay here. I will go upstairs, give it to them, and come back." At the lab, a tech asked for the patient's name.

"Resham Lal Bhandari," I said. He made a name tag and stuck it onto the little tube, then directed me to a corner of the room. "Put it there." After that, he asked me to pay him seven dollars for the lab test.

"When will the report come out?" I asked him while handing him the bills from my wallet.

"Might be four or five days," he said, counting the cash I gave him, and he handed me a receipt with the date on which I would come and pick up the report. It was Sunday of next week. I had to return with the same receipt in order to get the report. One my way back downstairs, I ran into Dr. Bikalp in the hallway.

"Dr. Saap, the report will take another few days to come out. My *sasuraba* is in a lot of pain. Isn't there medicine he can take to relieve his pain? Can you please recommend something?" I kindly asked.

"Please come to my general ward at noon, and I will prescribe the medicine," he said. I thought he could have prescribed the medications right then and there, but because we had to go to his ward, we had to purchase another ticket.

There were a few other patients who were waiting for Dr. Bikalp. The literal translation of Bikalp in Nepali is "alternative," and I wondered if he was the only "Bikalp" for us to save my *sasuraba* from this pain. Dr. Bikalp arrived one hour after the appointment time he had given us. I skipped in front of the other patients and entered his room. He prescribed the medication on a piece of plain paper and said, "The name of this medicine is morphine. I have prescribed 10 mg morphine tablets and a syrup. Please bring this to the hospital accountant's cabin and get a stamp, without which you cannot buy it. The pharmacists are not allowed to sell it without the official stamp. Have your *sasuraba* take the tablets twice a day and the syrup whenever he complains of pain."

The medicine he prescribed was only available in certain pharmacies that were authorized to sell it. They would only issue the exact amount as prescribed. The medicine Dr. Bikalp prescribed would last only for ten days.

"It will take almost five days for the biopsy test report. I don't think it makes sense for us to stay here. If I go to Pokhara, I can be with my daughters and neighbors. I will feel a lot better," my father-in-law said, twisting and writhing in pain. "I can take the medicine in the meantime. You can be here in Kathmandu to collect the report and to keep me updated. If I need to come back, I will do so. I would rather go to Pokhara. What do you think?"

I found his argument logical. His eyes had brightened at the thought.

Laxman *dai* nodded in approval.

"Sure, if you think so," I said. "I'll wait here for the report and keep you updated."

I helped him into the car. His hands trembled slightly as he settled into the seat. I forced a smile and stepped back.

As they pulled away, I stood there for a moment, blinking back the sting in my eyes. My phone ringing took my attention.

"What's up?" Kripa asked me.

"Not much," I said. "Your father and Laxman *dai* just left for Pokhara. He was relieved ... like being home might help him feel better."

"Really!" she said, her voice mixed with joy and sadness. "What did the doctor say?"

I explained everything about the plan for me to wait for the report. I only omitted the part about her father's real diagnosis.

Kripa felt satisfied. Although I knew the truth, I simply couldn't speak it.

"I've came out of seclusion but will not eat salty food until we finish the thirteen days of mourning. Suman *didi* said she would stay in the room until then. The priest allowed me to do so because I must breastfeed Krisha," she said, sounding more like herself, as if she had finally accepted her mother's death. However, her voice still lacked any joy or hope for life. I asked her about Krisha's health and whereabouts. I felt content and ended the call, then took a bus home to Tikathali. The day was over. I didn't feel like doing anything before bed.

Laxman *dai* informed me that they had made it to Pokhara at nine in the evening.

The weight of the new medication brought me a flicker of relief, knowing my father-in-law would endure less pain, yet it felt like a fragile comfort against the relentless advance of his disease. I could almost see the shadow of his illness, slowly consuming him, and the thought knotted my stomach.

Suman *didi* and Kripa had already faced so much heartache; the last thing I wanted was to add to their burden by revealing the harsh reality of their father's condition. The need to protect them felt like a double-edged sword—while I shielded them, I was also trapped in a cage of silence.

Every time I suppressed the truth, a wave of mental anguish crashed over me, each surge more suffocating than the last. It was as if I was carrying an unbearable weight, one that throbbed with a sharp ache in my chest. I longed to release those bottled emotions, to share the burden of sorrow, yet I found myself trapped in a relentless cycle of denial and fear.

Each passing day felt like a countdown, a painful reminder of what lay ahead. I wished I could face the reality instead of waiting in this limbo, but the fear of their anguish kept me rooted in silence, waiting for the inevitable moment when the truth would finally surface.

Chapter Eight

Another Witness to the End

December 6, 2019

My return ticket to America was booked for January 10. I had already been in Nepal for ten days, but everything I'd hoped to do—celebrate Krisha's birthday, spend time with my family—had been overshadowed by loss.

Kripa and Krisha were the ones I felt sorriest for. Losing a mother, and now bracing for the loss of a father—that was more than any heart should carry.

My five-day mourning rite was over. I hadn't eaten salt, as tradition required, and I had eight more days without meat. My body felt weak from the restriction, and the cravings had been strong—but I kept the promise. Out of love for Kripa.

I didn't feel like eating or drinking anything. It was nearly lunchtime when I finally left my bed. I sat down in the library, surrounded by the books I had collected over the years—some from high school, still lined with pencil marks from nights of struggle. They felt like small anchors to who I'd been, long before all this.

A few minutes later, my mother called me to lunch. We sat together in the kitchen. Lentil soup, rice, and beans—simple, familiar, unchanged.

I used a spoon out of habit after years in America. Otherwise, I would always use my hands to eat food while in Nepal. As I was about to put a first spoonful into my mouth, my mother's eyes met mine.

"You wear a troubled face. What has you stressed?"

"Nothing much. I have a headache," I said.

I stared at the plate and moved the spoon around to shovel on the rice.

"Do not stress out too much. Whatever has to happen will happen. Nothing is in our control. What else could be more tragic than this? But we should accept it," my mother said, repeating the same platitude everyone offers when it comes to comforting people. "Add more soup to the rice. It's dry."

"I am fine," I said, pouring some soup from the bowl onto the plate.

"And what did the doctor say about your father-in-law?" my father asked as he was eating rice.

"He has cancer," I replied without a second thought.

"What?" both my parents blurted out, with their mouths agape. The food in their hands remained suspended between their mouths and the plate.

"Nothing can be more tragic than this." I couldn't finish eating all the food on the plate. I went back to my own library.

I was still not sure what kind of cancer my father-in-law had. I went back to his results and flipped through the papers and various other medical reports. I also viewed the CT scan from the Imaging Center and read the words "Androgenic Cancer" in the report. I googled the word on my laptop.

I realized it was an end-stage cancer. The tumor in his pancreas had become bigger than normal, and it was expanding into other areas. I confirmed a hundred times that it was cancer. Although I knew it was cancer and the doctor had confirmed the diagnosis, it was hard for me to accept.

I thought of Kripa and the loss she already had suffered, coupled with her father's condition. My love for Kripa overwhelmed me. Kripa always stood by my side and accepted my troubles as her own. I knew her plight was more painful than what any person should endure. *I must be by her side.* I wanted to hear her voice, so I called her with many questions. "How are you? What are you doing? Did you have your meal?"

"Yes, I did. And you?"

"I'm finished now and I'm looking at the computer. And how is Krisha doing?"

"She also had some food, and now she is at the *fupudidi's* house."

"Okay, don't allow yourself to get too stressed. Make sure you take care of your health too. And how is your father's pain now?"

"After taking the morphine, he says the pain is not too bad and he slept well last night," she replied. Her voice sounded relaxed, reassuring.

"That's good. At least he managed to sleep," I said, relieved. "I will keep in touch with the doctors. Please let me know if there is any more pain."

"Okay. When will you come to Shishuwa?" she asked, her voice aching with longing.

When she said *"I miss you,"* something in me softened. After the loss of her mother, those words carried more than affection—they were an offering, fragile and full of grace.

A rush of tenderness surged in me. I wanted to hold her, to press my face into the curve of her neck, to kiss away all that had been taken.

"Soon," I said, my voice warm with promise. "As soon as I get the FNA report. But know that I miss you more."

We hung up.

And the silence returned.

The more stressful things became, the more powerless I felt to protect her. I lay on the bed, eyes fixed on the ceiling, my thoughts stalled. No answers. Just a weight in my chest and the hum of uncertainty.

In the corner, a spider's web shimmered faintly in the light. A fly zipped into its threads and struggled for a breath of time—then stilled.

Another death. Another small, cruel ending.

I thought of Woolf's moth, its wings tapping the windowpane, pulsing with the desire to live. She pitied its limits. I understood.

My own life felt caught—hovering between grief and the aching wish to move forward.

I closed my eyes and contemplated the situation. I had to go to the teaching hospital on Sunday to get my father-in-law's FNA biopsy report. I lay on the bed for a while with my eyes open. My head felt heavy. I thought about Krisha and how I missed her. I had no time to spend with her, nor she with us. Overwhelmed by emotions, I buried my face in my hands, desperately trying to stifle the urge to cry, to conceal my pain from the world.

Chapter Nine

Ph.D. Title and the Rising Darkness

December 8, 2019

It was the ninth day after my mother-in-law's passing. Although my wife was no longer in seclusion, she still was not eating salty food. There were still four more days until Suman *didi* could come out of seclusion, when the mourning days would be over.

I had to go get my father-in-law's FNA report.

After finishing my morning chores, I took the bus from Tikathali to Koteshwor, then boarded a Nepal Yatayat headed for the teaching hospital. I arrived by nine and showed the receipt from our last visit. Then I waited in the General Ward for Dr. Bikalp.

He was supposed to arrive at ten but didn't. I paced the corridor, asked assistants about his whereabouts, explained the urgency. One doctor gave me his number and advised I text rather than call.

I did.

"Namaste, Dr. Saap," I wrote. "I'm the same person who brought his father-in-law from Pokhara—the patient with pancreatic, androgenic cancer. You had asked me to bring his report today. I'm here now, waiting in the General Ward. If you could come soon and review it, I'll be able to return to Pokhara today. Kind regards, Tulasi Acharya, Ph.D."

I added the Ph.D.—not out of vanity, but hope. If he saw me as a fellow professional, he might respond faster.

He did.

"I will be in the General Ward within fifteen minutes."

I waited, fingers crossed, hoping for a miracle—that *Sasuraba* didn't have cancer at all.

Dr. Bikalp arrived nearly a half hour later.

As soon as I saw him, I slipped into the ward and told the patients ahead of me, "I need to show him this report—I'll be quick." I hated jumping the line, but in Nepal, that kind of thing was common. In America, people waited their turn. But here, sometimes urgency outweighed order.

Still, I reminded myself, every culture has its strengths. Nepal, too, had its virtues—its deep-rooted traditions, its resilience, its sense of community.

"Let me see the report," Dr. Bikalp said, as he reached for the papers.

"Is this really cancer, Dr. Saap?" I asked, acting as if I didn't know anything about it. I was hoping for a miracle, that it would turn out not to be cancer.

He raised his eyes from the report and directed a perplexed gaze at me, furrowing his brow, which made me feel as though he regarded me as a fool.

"It is cancer," he said. "I already told you. No doubt on that. We wanted to see things in detail. Your father-in-law's condition is in the final stages, and he cannot be healed. Nor can we extend his longevity any further."

His words sent a chilling tremor through my spine.

"Can't we treat him? Would it be possible if we brought him to another bigger hospital in India or so?" was my immediate reaction to his reply.

"If you were to bring him to a top hospital in America or India, your father-in-law's chances of recovery are slim," he said.

He stared into my eyes with an unwavering gaze that carried the weight of truth. It came across as harsh and rude, but deep down, I knew it was the bitterness of reality. The truth often carries a harshness and bluntness that can be difficult to bear. At that moment, however, I found myself trembling within, unable to process the magnitude of the truth unfolding before me.

Thoughts raced through my mind, questioning the circumstances that led to this suffering. What had he done in his past life to endure such a fate? What mistakes had his daughters made to face this tragedy? These haunting questions assaulted my thoughts, leaving me feeling overwhelmed and unable to find solace. I felt a lump forming in my throat, which rendered me speechless. All that escaped my lips were coughs and the sound of clearing my throat, as if the weight of the situation had shattered my ability to communicate effectively.

"Wherever you take him, the treatment process and the methods are the same," he added, his voice straining toward kindness.

His eyes lingered on my face—drawn, heavy, flushed with despair.

"However, I have some more advice. I am not hopeful, but you may try. Go see Dr. Ambuj Karna at Bir Hospital. Whatever he suggests, do it."

I came to understand that, in the most despairing circumstances, the presence of hope endured, perhaps as an inherent law of nature.

I went straight to Bir Hospital, catching a microbus that would take me there. It was a little after lunch by then. I rushed to the ticket counter of the hospital and asked about Dr. Karna's schedule.

One of the women working at the counter said, "He will be here on Monday and Wednesday—Monday from nine in the morning to one in the afternoon, and Wednesday from one to four in the afternoon."

I decided to come back the next morning. Ratnapark wasn't far, so I walked to catch the next bus. The area was always buzzing—a collision of politics, poverty, and street life. Once a gathering place for hunger strikes and protest speeches, now it was also home to retirees killing time, vendors shouting their prices, and sex workers slipping through the crowd, hoping not to be noticed by the police.

I passed the park without stopping, aware of the chaos but untouched by it. My thoughts were elsewhere.

I got on the microbus and reached Naya Baneswor, where I waited for another bus, Shubhakamana Yatayat, which would go to Tikathali. I waited for a long time, but I didn't see the bus coming, so I stopped by the tea stand and lit a cigarette to kill time.

I sucked in and puffed out. *This might also cause cancer*, I thought to myself.

"Forget about it! There is no guarantee of who dies when!" I talked to myself while smoking the cigarette. "Anyway, I don't smoke every day."

Just then I saw the Shubhakamana Yatayat coming toward the bus stop. I tossed the cigarette butt and got in. There were enough seats for me to take one. Usually, it's very rare to find an empty seat on public transportation in Kathmandu.

I sat down and called my wife to update her. "I have to go see Dr. Ambuj Karna tomorrow at Bir Hospital. Dr. Bikalp recommends him." I asked her about Krisha's whereabouts and my father-in-law's condition. Asking had become my daily routine, sometimes twice a day.

"After taking morphine, he sleeps well, but he says that at times he has unbearable pain," Kripa said. "Please ask the doctor why he still has pain with all the medicine he is taking."

"I will," I said, and we hung up.

By then I had already reached the Tikathali bus station. I got off the bus and walked home. I put my backpack on the chair in the library and went straight to my bedroom to lie down. It was still light outside, but I felt dark and exhausted. I longed to see Kripa, and especially Krisha whose birthday was fast approaching. We were in the midst of a situation that rendered any thought of a birthday celebration a distant dream.

Chapter Ten

The Riddle of Palliative Care

December 9, 2019

During my time in Nepal, I visited many doctors, both with my father-in-law and without him, and they all said his disease was incurable. At first, I refused to believe it. I thought the first two may have been mistaken, that they lacked expertise or had misread the scans. It was when I visited that last doctor, Dr. Karna, that I finally had to face the truth. We could go through with chemotherapy, but ultimately, he would die anyway.

At this appointment, I learned what palliative care meant. It wasn't about curing—it was about comfort. About helping someone live as peacefully as possible when time was short and pain was constant. Three months, or a little more. It was measured not in days but in dignity.

Later, I researched it. The World Health Organization called it "an approach that improves the quality of life of patients and their families ... through the prevention and relief of suffering." But I didn't need a definition. I had seen the suffering. I was living the question of how to ease it.

Dr. Karna, a man in his mid-forties with a youthful appearance, possessed a strong physique evident in his broad shoulders, as if he worked out regularly. His face was elongated, with hair neatly combed back, and his demeanor was both friendly and composed, as reflected in his smiling countenance and soothing tone of voice. He took the time to thoroughly explain everything to me.

"Dr. Saap, I have not yet mentioned to his daughter that he has cancer. He does not have a son, only daughters, who are now in mourning as I said. I don't have the courage to share this with them, to cause another tragedy in the family. I am the one supporting them now," I blurted out.

Dr. Karna listened to me attentively, as if he were a close friend.

"I am sorry to hear all that. We can do as much as we can do. Nothing is in our control. You'll have to break the news to the family sooner or later; the sooner the better. I am still around forty percent hopeful that if your father-in-law starts chemo, we can extend his life expectancy. If possible, I want to see the patient. You don't have to tell his daughters about their father's disease yet, but bring him here and let me examine him."

Dr. Karna's words ignited a profound sense of hope within me, dispelling the despair that had consumed my thoughts about my *sasuraba's* health and the possibility of finding a cure. Each word he uttered resonated deeply, creating a harmonious symphony of hope that broke through the gloomy clouds that overshadowed my mind. His voice seemed to carry a magical melody, infusing my spirit with renewed vitality and breathing life into my troubled body. In that fleeting moment, despair gave way to a spirited optimism.

"Sure, Dr. Saap. Thank you," I said, nodding in approval. "By the way, my father-in-law said that he still has pain though he is taking morphine."

I remembered what Kripa had said. I showed him the medication Dr. Bikalp had prescribed.

"Dr. Bikalp said that after taking this medicine, my father-in-law wouldn't have pain, but he is still in pain."

"This is the right drug. If he's still in pain, let's increase the dose," Dr. Karna said in a calm tone, looking at the medicine prescribed. "It's only 10 mg. Let's make it 20 mg now. I will prescribe more syrup and paracetamol. Increase the dose and have him drink the syrup anytime he has pain, and take three tablets of paracetamol every eight hours."

He handed me the prescription, saying, "Don't forget to get the official stamp so you can purchase this medicine at the counter."

"Thank you very much, Dr. Saap," I said, trying to get up from the chair. "And what should we do if he isn't ready for chemo?"

"If so, keep increasing the dose whenever he's in pain," he said. "There's no other option." He paused. "If you decide to start chemo, don't delay. The longer we wait, the worse it gets. But first—I need to see the patient."

He stared at me, his tone more official now.

"Bring his citizenship papers when you come. The government can help with treatment costs, but we need the ID to apply. An oncologist has to write a formal recommendation letter with all the patient's details."

"Sure, Dr. Saap. Can you please prescribe more medicine at least for fifteen days in case we need time to make it here?"

"You cannot buy that much of these medicines at once. The pharmacist won't allow you more than ten days. When you run out of them, come and see me, and I will prescribe more. Do not worry. I am here for you."

"Sure. Thank you so much, Dr. Saap."

I walked out of his office with a heavy heart but a faint sense of possibility. Dr. Karna was a very good doctor who showed kindness and spoke in calm, sympathetic tones about my father-in-law's situation. Most importantly, he raised hope that we wouldn't need to give up. Still, I was in a dilemma, wondering how I could do all those things without letting him and his family know. This dilemma started eating at my mind, churning in my belly. Although the weather outside was cold, I could feel the sweat beading on my forehead. It was noon.

Kripa called. "Where are you?" she asked. "Have you met Dr. Ambuj Karna?"

"I am leaving his office. He wants to see the patient."

I tried to sound hopeful.

"We should bring him in after the thirteen days of mourning," I said.

Kripa responded with excitement and urged me to proceed. I knew, however, that breaking the news about chemotherapy would be the hardest part. To shift the focus, I asked about Krisha. She was sleeping.

As I wrapped up the call, I told her I would video call once I got home. After hanging up, I took a deep breath, feeling a sense of accomplishment.

I spent some time walking through the crowded streets, letting the noise of Kathmandu fill the space around me—the honking horns, the shrill whistles of traffic officers, the steady rhythm of hurried footsteps. People rushed past as if chasing something urgent, though I wondered if they knew what it was.

We all walk that way sometimes—driven, distracted, uncertain.

Illness has a way of cutting through the noise. It reminds us what truly matters. Health, presence, the people we love. The rest—money, status, pride—feels flimsy by comparison. Like smoke rising from a cigarette.

I stopped at a tea stand and sipped a cup of black tea, a cigarette between my fingers, thinking about life and its illusions, about the strange truths we only seem to understand when we're standing too close to loss.

After I got home, I video called Kripa.

"Show me, Krisha," I said.

She turned the camera, and I switched to a toddler's tone. "What is my daughter doing? I see you."

Krisha was still learning to speak. I longed to scoop her up, to sing to her, to hold her close—but she barely knew me. I had come to Nepal with dreams of bonding with her, of becoming her father in more than name only. But so far, I hadn't had the chance. She viewed me through the screen like I was a stranger, her face twisting as if she might cry.

I missed her more than I knew how to say.

In a few weeks, I was due back in the U.S. for the start of my semester. But how could I leave now? Kripa was grieving her mother. My father-in-law was slipping away. And Krisha—our baby—still needed both of us.

I felt torn in every direction, as if my head might burst from the pressure.

"I have a terrible headache," I told Kripa. "I'll talk to you before bed. Right now, I need to rest."

I hung up the phone.

By nightfall, I felt a quiet surge of anticipation. I would see Kripa. I would hold Krisha. That thought lifted me—if only for a moment.

Grief was a weight, but hope moved like light between the cracks.

Chapter Eleven

Pollution, Pranayama, and Profession

December 10, 2019

I woke to the sound of barking street dogs at five o'clock. My mind still buzzed with uncertainty, but something had shifted. The grief and fear were still there, pressing at the edges, but beneath them, a quiet resolve had begun to grow.

I rolled out of bed and onto the carpet, settling into Anulom Vilom—a type of Pranayama, the ancient yogic practice of breath control. Inhale, exhale, one breath at a time. It was the first time in weeks I'd done yoga without distraction. Outside, Kathmandu's air hung heavy with pollution, muffling the city in a toxic haze. But here, inside this small room, I reclaimed a sliver of clarity.

As I breathed, I thought of Kripa's voice from the night before—strained but steady. We had spoken about her father's pain, the medications I'd picked up, the nearing end of the mourning period. The words had been similar to previous conversations, but the undercurrent was different. We were no longer circling our sorrow. We were preparing to act.

My phone buzzed again. A new message from her: "Call when you can."

There were no declarations this time, no desperate I miss yous. Just a thread stretched quietly between us, tugging me forward.

After a short call and shared silence, I turned to my laptop. The blinking cursor awaited me, just as it had the day before. I tried to focus on preparing the new curriculum for the college's Professional, Business, and Technical Writing program—a position I was proud to have earned. But my attention drifted. I had the credentials, the job title, the to-do list. Yet nothing about my current life resembled professional success. I wasn't even sure who I was in this moment—a teacher, a father, a caretaker, a son?

I turned on the heater against the morning chill, but no warmth could soothe the ache of divided purpose.

Later, I told my parents I would travel to Pokhara the next day. They nodded with understanding, though their concern hung quietly in the air. My mother reminded me to pack everything I'd need—medicine, documents, clothes. Her voice was gentle, but her eyes searched mine.

I busied myself with errands—sorting papers, checking supplies, tying up the details of the journey ahead. But my thoughts kept drifting to Krisha. Her tiny hands. Her face twisting in confusion during video calls. I hoped she'd smile when she saw me again. I hoped she'd know who I was.

The sun dipped low behind the haze. Through the smogged window, I watched the traffic crawl past. Scooters, buses, rickshaws—each carrying someone rushing toward something urgent. And yet the urgency inside me felt different. It was not a chase. It was a return.

I was leaving in the morning. Not because I had all the answers. But because some promises can't be postponed.

I zipped up the same bag I'd carried across two continents. It felt heavier this time—not with things, but with truths I couldn't ignore.

Chapter Twelve

Power of Poetry

December 11, 2019

Today was Krisha's birthday. A rhythm danced in my chest as thoughts of seeing her again—of seeing Kripa—filled my mind.

I packed light: a few clothes, my laptop—my lifeline for teaching, grading, writing, earning. A few books slipped in too. New Nepali releases like *Antardrishti* by Kamal Lamichhane, *Grandmothers' Stories* by Amrita Lamsal, *Hansh* by Sanjeev Upreti. I added a couple of unread Madan Prize winners and, tucked between them, an old anthology of romantic poets.

William Blake's voice has followed me since school days. Back then, I would read the poetry first from the *Mahendra Mala* (Nepali textbook) before my father had time to wrap them in protective covers.

I caught a bus from Tikathali to Kalanki, where microbuses lined up like restless cattle, ready to leave the valley. I bought a five-dollar ticket to Pokhara. Kathmandu's air had turned colder, so I pulled a woolen hat over my ears, feeling the bite ease slightly as the bus began to move.

I reached for the poetry book. As the city blurred past the window, I turned its pages and found Blake's *Sunflower*—a poem I'd returned to again and again.

Ah Sun-flower! weary of time,   *Who countest the steps of the Sun:*
Seeking after that sweet golden clime   *Where the traveller's journey is done...*

Poetry ached for rest—for peace—for reunion.

The poem reminded me of Kripa, still aching from her mother's death. Blake's sunflower reached for a golden land where the journey ends—and I thought of the *Vedas*, of the body returning to earth, the soul carrying on. *In the end, who escapes death? No one. We move forward, because the world does, too.*

At Nagdhunga, the gateway out of the valley, folk songs blared from the bus speakers. Some passengers grumbled, others asked for Hindi tunes. I tucked the poetry book away and pulled out *Chhapamarako Choro*. The opening pages drew me in, but the weight of it—stories of war and loss—felt too close.

I thought of *Palpasa Café*, Narayan Wagle's novel about the Maoist conflict, and its rise beyond Nepal's borders. How do we carry such stories into the world? Can they speak for us, or only reflect on what's already broken?

I put *Chhaapaamarako Choro* back and took out Lamichhane's *Anatrdrishti*. By then, the microbus had passed Thankot and stopped at a food court for breakfast. I ate some fried peas and smoked a cigarette while sipping black tea. When travelling, I usually tended to smoke, but it also depended on my mood. Sometimes I didn't. While in America, I never smoked because I couldn't buy one cigarette without buying the whole pack. It was expensive. And it would cost me more in terms of health if I bought a whole pack and ended up smoking more at once.

After breakfast, the driver floored the gas on the microbus, and I worried that the bus might veer off the winding road. I started reading *Antardrishti*, flipping through its pages, wondering how Lamichhane, who lost both of his eyes, managed to complete his Ph.D. He worked in the field of research at JAICA (Japan International Cooperation Company) in Japan and then at Harvard University in the United States. I found the book inspirational as it described his childhood, education, his ups and downs and how he pursued his career.

The book made interesting points about his own experiences and how society viewed people with disabilities. It discussed how society couldn't progress until we changed the way we perceived each other and the world. I had written my Ph.D. dissertation on women with disabilities, which might explain why I enjoyed this book and read it with much interest.

I finished the book during the six-hour bus ride, choosing not to get off at the lunch stop. When I arrived at my father-in-law's house in Sisuwa Chowk around one in the afternoon, Suman *didi* was still in seclusion. Two days remained before the thirteen-day mourning period would end.

Kripa was sitting on the veranda with her father. Krisha played nearby, toddling between them. It was her birthday—a day I'd once imagined with cake, candles, and songs. But now, in mourning, I could only watch her in silence and whisper the wish in my heart.

Tears welled up—hot, sudden, uninvited. I wiped them away before anyone could see.

Neighbors and relatives moved in and out of the house. No one greeted one another; during mourning *namaste* was forbidden. I caught Kripa's gaze—her eyes red-rimmed, her face pale, her lips dry and tight. Her spirit worn, hollowed by grief. But when she saw me, something in her softened.

Krisha didn't acknowledge me. I knelt and called to her, but she ran to her grandfather.

"Baa ... baa ..." she said, her tiny voice full of affection.

It pierced me. But I had been gone. She didn't know me yet. That wasn't her fault.

Still, I watched her, and in the sound of her laughter, I found something like comfort.

"How are you feeling now, *Buwa*? I asked my father-in-law.

"Same o' same, *Jwaisaap*. I was able to sleep after taking morphine. That's it. Pain is the same at times. But getting some sleep is the biggest thing to celebrate for me now," he said while still pressing his belly to ease the pain. He stretched out his body.

I took out the medicine from my backpack and asked Kripa to put it safely away. I gestured to my father-in-law: "The doctor said we should increase the dose so you have less pain and more sleep. You also should take paracetamol three times a day, three pills each time."

"Okay, I will start taking them tomorrow," he said. I chatted with him for a while.

Outside the veranda, the vehicles passed by noisily on the road. The bells in the temples rang, and a few birds flew off from the electric wires they were perched on.

"See the bird," I said to Krisha, pointing toward them to draw her attention and hoping that Krisha might come to me, but she didn't care. She again ran to her grandfather. All my efforts were in vain. I felt so lonely and abandoned. I felt hurt. My heart filled with love for Krisha. I felt as if I had lost Krisha's love for me because I had been absent for so long. I thought about leaving America and staying with my daughter.

It was Kripa, Krisha, Suman *didi*, Jaya *dai*, my father-in-law, and myself in the house, along with Suman *didi's* two children. In the evening, some neighbors came to attend the *kriyapurti*, the mourners living in the secluded area of the house.

Chapter Thirteen

Hollow Body on a Faded Couch

December 12, 2019

The living room walls were lined with memories—framed photos Kripa had arranged weeks before her mother passed. Her parents on a bench. A family portrait. Pictures of Suman *didi* and her children. One of Kripa and me. Another from last year's trip to Kusma, all of us grinning beneath the cloudy sky.

Zenith's montage stood out—his life from birth to five, frozen in color. He was twelve now, taller, more reserved. Kripa loved her sister's children deeply—sometimes, I thought, more than herself.

The TV buzzed in the background, as always. It was her father's constant companion, on whether he was in the room or not. The screen flickered endlessly until he went to bed.

He sat slouched on the red couch, its cushions faded and thin from years of use. His body smaller now, as if the fabric might swallow him whole.

"I love this couch more than my bed and feel great when I lie here," he used to say. They had bought the couch ten years ago.

It felt like my father-in-law had spent ten years of his life sitting in and being around that couch. After he became sick, he was glued to the couch. Not only was it faded and worn out, but its legs were rotten and eaten by wood worms. There were holes everywhere, as if it might break at any moment, an apt metaphorical representation of my *sasuraba*'s current condition.

The couch had its own story to tell. Kripa had shared it with me one day. "Any men who came to our house looking for a bride might take it as a bad sign that we didn't have a couch to sit on, so I thought it would be a good idea to buy one. I purchased it with the money I made from my journalism career."

After that, many boys came to see her, but she didn't like any of them.

"They avoided my gaze, and I didn't hear any manliness in their voice," she told me once. "After you came into my life, everything changed. You were the type of person I was looking for who was supportive of my career and encouraged me all the time, saying 'you should be in the profession you like, and you must be who you are.' That impressed me."

I absorbed the room one more time, as if some mystery was hidden there, and my job was to uncover it. I thought about all those pictures slowly disappearing. The memories of those who passed away would continue to disappear as the colors in the photos faded.

I took a deep breath and wondered how to tell Suman *didi* and Kripa the truth.

Their father had cancer. There was no way around it now. Dr. Karna had offered a sliver of hope—chemo might buy him time—but saying the word *chemo* would make everything real.

I replayed the dilemma in my mind like a loop with no end. *How do you break news like that? How do you say it out loud, knowing it can't be unsaid?*

I lay back on the bed, staring at the ceiling, thinking of all the ways fate could have rewritten this. What if it had been him instead of her? My *sasuma*, always so strong, gone without warning—while her husband now sat fading, day by day.

Grief doesn't follow logic. It only leaves questions behind.

Today was the twelfth day since my mother-in-law had passed away.

The neighbors and relatives began to gather at the house. In a display of solidarity deeply rooted in Nepali culture, they offered their assistance willingly. They diligently cleaned the house, washed clothes, swept the floors, and graciously served tea to the visiting guests and other individuals who came to pay their respects. Such acts of communal support and cooperation are ingrained in the fabric of our society, emphasizing the importance of helping one another during times of need.

It's hard not to contrast this support with the typical response in a different cultural context, such as in America, where considerations of monetary value and time spent may hold greater prominence. The difference lies not in the willingness to help, but rather in the varying ways that support and assistance are extended and valued.

The next day would be the thirteenth day of my *sasuma's* passing, so the neighbors started dividing the work duty. I thought I should perhaps talk about my father-in-law's condition with Jaya *dai*. Someone brought tea on a serving plate, and I took a cup and sipped it. By now everyone was up, and most of them had entered the living room.

"*Dai*, after we finish drinking tea, we should go downstairs. I have to talk to you," I said to Jaya *dai* while taking a sip.

"Okay," he said.

After we finished the tea, we went downstairs and sat by the temple floor, leaning against the building's pole.

"*Dai*, I've found out that our father-in-law's disease won't be cured. I met with multiple doctors, and all of them said the same thing based on the CT scan report," I said.

"What happened? What did the doctors say?" he asked in shocked tones. His jaw dropped and forehead puckered with concern.

"He has pancreatic cancer," I said, without hesitation.

Jaya *dai* was speechless. He could only shake his head. A silence descended on us. Only the tong-tong sound of the bell at the temple echoed, as if to sound another death. A few women came to the tap by the temple to fill their pots with water. The gush of water filling the pots filled our ears. Some sparrows flew and perched on the electric wire overhead, then flew away. A motorcycle passed by, horn honking. Finally, I broke the silence.

"But Dr. Karna has some hope that chemo might help him extend his life, though he cannot guarantee it. It depends whether our father-in-law can tolerate the chemo or not."

When the doctor first talked about chemo, I had come home and googled it. Mayo Clinic defined it as "a drug treatment that uses powerful chemicals to kill fast-growing cells in your body." I also knew that while chemotherapy is effective, it is not without risks, as it may result in side effects ranging from mild and manageable to more severe complications.

Jaya *dai* was staring at the corner without any words to share, speechless.

"What can we do now, *dai*? Dr. has asked me to bring the patient for chemo," I said, breaking the silence again. "I am not sure how I would break this news to Kripa and Suman *didi*. Laxman *dai* knows this, but I have told him not to tell anyone about it."

Jaya *dai* woke from his daze. He burst out in anger.

"What the hell is this, man? It's happening to this family again? One after another. If he had cancer, I'm sure he would have rather passed away instead of his healthy wife."

His thoughts echoed my own.

"I think we must let Kripa and Suman *didi* know about the chemo option. We need to hear their opinions. We cannot let their father know, but we must tell the daughters. What do you think?" I asked, leaning against a pole. My back was killing me from the long bus ride.

"We can tell them, but let's wait until the thirteenth day is over tomorrow. Let's finish and wrap up the rites first, then we can discuss this and move ahead accordingly."

We got up and went straight to our chores, preparing for the next day. I tried to play with Krisha—she was on the veranda with her cousin Araju—but she bolted the moment she saw me. I turned to my father-in-law instead. He showed little pain this morning, though the years of torment were still carved into his face.

Trying to lift his spirits without revealing the truth, I added a touch of humor. "You're looking strong today," I said. "When do you think we'll finally fulfill your wish, father? Remember how you used to talk about getting drunk on whiskey and feasting on venison?"

He smiled—an honest smile, but I could see what it cost him.

I was the only one who saw the weight behind it: the pain he carried, the trials still ahead, the pressure building inside him. And I knew the silence wouldn't last. Sooner or later, the truth would break through—loud and undeniable, echoing through all of us.

Chapter Fourteen

Celebration of Death

December 13, 2019

All the relatives and neighbors started arriving at the house in the morning. The Bhandari family in Sisuwa area was large, so it was not difficult for all of them to manage doing the chores—some of them started cleaning the house while others cooked, chopped vegetables, and gathered items for the priest. It was the thirteenth day of my mother-in-law's passing.

On the thirteenth day of mourning, it is said that the family should invite all the relatives and neighbors who were present on the day of the death. They should be fed and allowed to stay until they were fully satisfied. Otherwise, the soul of the dead body won't rest in peace. It was an important ritual. All those gathered in the house started talking, chatting, enjoying themselves as if they were at a celebration. The one who had died was dead and gone. But those who survive must continue to live their lives. Is death a celebration? I considered this. Some of them had already set up an oven and lit a fire on the top floor. Others started chopping cauliflower, while some set themselves to cooking, boiling things in big pots, cracking jokes, and talking to people around as if no one had died and everything was back to normal.

On the floor I could see the beans, brinjal, bitter gourd, and leafy vegetables my mother-in-law had planted. They were still green and loaded with flowers and fruits. She had tended them with manure and water. I saw her image lingering in the leaves of those fresh green vegetables, though she had died thirteen days ago.

Smiles, joy, and celebration usually have no place after a death because to do so at such a time might be considered cruel, rude, and barbaric. But the thirteenth day of my sasuma's death helped me understand and acknowledge her death and learn how to accept it and move on in life. Many western societies consider death as a farewell from life. Mexicans believe in revisiting the dead, so they carry food and water with them and go to the tomb, waiting for the dead to return. Indonesians keep the dead body in their house for a long time. They repeatedly dig up and view the body after burial. In Madagascar, they dig up the dead body every seven years, wrap it in new cloth, and bury it once again. In Sri Lanka, they continue to weep in mourning for a month when an immediate family member dies. Even more interesting, if they are unable to weep for so long, they hire someone to weep for them. These people are called "rudali." But in Hindu culture, when the body is burned and cremated, it is gone forever, and the soul is believed to rest either in Heaven or Hell depending on the deeds of the person during life.

The thirteenth day after my *sasuma's* passing provided me some solace in my contemplation of death as an integral part of life. In her article "Death doesn't need our respect. Let's celebrate life at funerals," published in *The Guardian* on July 18, 2018, Erica Buist explores the notion that every being is both experiencing birth and inching closer to death simultaneously. Buist suggests that acknowledging the equal importance of birth and death can lead to a perspective where death is embraced, celebrated, and devoid of fear. However, when faced with the reality of a death within one's immediate family, putting such concepts into practice proves to be a far more challenging task.

Indeed, various perspectives and philosophies regard death as a transformation or a reunion of the soul with something eternal. The Hindu holy book *Shreebhagbat Gita* also delves into the concept of death. In the second chapter, the 20th stanza emphasizes that the soul is neither born nor does it die. It has always existed, transcending the notions of birth and death. The lines below reveal that the immortal nature of the soul remains unaffected by the death of the physical body:

Na jayate mriyate wa kadachina
Naya bhutwaa bhawitaa wa na bhuya
Ajo nitya: shashwatyoya purano
Na hanyate hanyamane sharire
It is never born or nor does it die
It has never been, nor will it ever be again.
Soul is always immortal—
It is not killed with the body's death.

This profound understanding suggests that the soul is everlasting and untouchable. However, despite possessing this knowledge, when faced with death within one's immediate family, the emotional impact can be overwhelming. The profound grief and personal loss make it challenging to fully embrace these abstract concepts surrounding death. The real-life experience of losing a loved one reminds us of the depth of our human emotions, which can be difficult to reconcile with intellectual or philosophical ideas.

The priest, who had been invited to perform the thirteenth-day death ritual, successfully completed his sacred duties, leading the fire worship and reciting mantras from the sacred texts. Following this, he proceeded to mark our foreheads with yellow-colored tika, symbolizing auspiciousness and protection. With the rituals concluded, we all gathered to share a meal, which brought about a sense of unity and closure.

As the meal came to an end, our relatives bid their farewells, content and uplifted by the shared experience. The completion of these rituals marked the symbolic end of the mourning period, providing a sense of fulfillment and peace as we prepared to resume our daily lives.

As the house emptied and silence descended once more, only Jaya *dai*, myself, Suman *didi*, Kripa, Krisha, Zenith, and Araju remained. The absence of my mother-in-law lingered in the room, heavy and undeniable, touching each of us in different ways. The void she left behind was palpable, and our hearts ached with a deep longing for her.

Her physical form had been transformed into ashes, scattered gently into the Seti River. All that remained were the pictures adorning the walls, capturing her essence and radiating the warmth of her smile. Suman *didi* and Kripa, overwhelmed by emotions, found peace in silent tears, their grief unspoken but deeply felt.

Meanwhile, my father-in-law sought comfort on his favorite red couch, taking his prescribed morphine to ease his pain. The clock showed it was already eight in the evening—a reminder of the passing hours and the somber atmosphere that surrounded us. In the midst of this solitude, we grappled with the bittersweet memories of the one who had departed, cherishing the moments captured in the photographs that now served as a poignant reminder of her presence in our lives.

We laid mattresses on the living room floor, choosing to sleep side by side, finding comfort in each other's presence. But in that shared space, I wrestled with whether to tell Kripa and Suman *didi* the truth. Their hearts were still raw from losing their mother. How could I burden them with more?

The doctor's words wouldn't leave me: their father had six months at most. No treatment could change that.

Yet, amidst this internal struggle, I thought of Dr. Karna's cautious optimism—that chemotherapy might still offer my s*asuraba* a little more life. The conflict consumed my thoughts and emotions, searing through me and leaving me paralyzed by indecision. The looming prospect of another thirteen-day mourning period intensified the pressure, but for now, I resolved to push these thoughts aside until the following day. Today marked the end of the mourning for my beloved *Sasuma*, and I desperately clung to that semblance of respite, hoping to find relief in the present moment.

Chapter Fifteen

Difficulty of Hiding the Truth

December 14, 2019

Two weeks had passed since that sorrowful Saturday when my *sasuma* had left her house, intending to accompany her husband for his treatment, only to suddenly collapse and meet her untimely demise due to a heart attack.

Kripa and Krisha were already seated on the veranda when I awoke. "You're up already?" I asked. "Why?" It was only seven o'clock, and the others were still slumbering peacefully. Curiosity piqued, I joined Kripa and Krisha on the veranda, seeking support in their presence.

"I didn't sleep well last night. I had a dream about my mother," Kripa shared in a somber tone, breastfeeding Krisha on her lap. The winter weather enveloped us with its cold and foggy embrace, mirroring the heaviness in our hearts. "I still can't fathom that my mother is gone. Sometimes, I wonder if the doctor declared her death without properly diagnosing her. Perhaps, if someone had been there with her, taking her to the hospital immediately, she might still be alive."

Turning to me, she continued, her voice filled with a mixture of grief and uncertainty, "What do you think, *Budho*? Do you believe the doctor pronounced her dead with breath left in her?" Kripa swallowed hard, her anguish palpable.

Witnessing her vulnerability, Krisha momentarily released her mouth from her mother's breast and gazed into Kripa's eyes, searching for sanctuary and understanding.

How could I answer? How could I predict? I had no response for her.

"Perhaps she had to die," Kripa mused, her voice trembled. "So, she decided to take me to the temple on my birthday last time and wished me good health. She gazed into my eyes with so much love and care, as if she were saying goodbye. Did she know that she was dying? Why didn't I sense her impending death?" she added, her sorrow deep.

"Kripa, if you start imagining nonsense and speaking gibberish, you will never be able to recover. We need to start looking toward the future, toward the living. If you continue down this path, you'll make me and our daughter sick," I said in a fit of emotion.

I immediately realized that she was only expressing her feelings, and I had responded rudely. There was no timeframe on grief. It was not a good idea to blame her for feeling sad, and it was certainly not true that she was making everyone around her ill. I hugged her tight, saying "sorry" and rubbing her back.

"How can I spend my life without thinking of her, *Budho*? With my mother gone, my life feels meaningless and absurd. I can't find any way to comfort myself," she said, her eyes reddening as she adjusted Krisha on her lap to a new breastfeeding position.

"What else is left for us but to think of her in our hearts? Let's think positively. At least she wasn't bedridden with a long illness, which would be like suffering death in life. We have seen many old and sick people who end up urinating and defecating in bed and living a miserable life as they waited for death. At least your mother had an easy death. Let's try to think of it that way. Perhaps she had done very good things in the past and was rewarded with an easy death."

I held her gaze as I tried to be positive and make her feel comfortable. Kripa's eyes became clouded with sadness, and tears streamed down her cheeks.

"If my father's health improves, it would help me to find the strength to carry on," Kripa continued, her voice quivering with emotion. She wiped away her tears and pinched the bridge of her nose, searching for clarity amid the chaos in her mind.

As Kripa expressed this sentiment, an overwhelming fear enveloped me as I considered how to confront her vulnerability. I made an effort to conceal my apprehension, not letting it show on my face. Silently, I questioned how I would reveal the truth about her father's illness, the mere thought of it suffocating me. Meanwhile, tractors loaded with pebbles and sand rumbled along the road, creating a cacophony of noise. The construction of concrete houses was underway on the opposite side of the street. Grocery store shutters were being raised, and the milkman went from door to door, distributing cartons of milk.

Shortly after, Suman *didi* woke up and joined us, greeting us with a cheerful "Good morning!" We exchanged morning pleasantries, briefly escaping the weight of our worries in those fleeting moments.

I resolved that I had to disclose the news about their father's illness to Kripa and Suman *didi*, no matter the cost. To broach the subject, I brought up the fact that Dr. Ambuj Karna expressed a desire to see their father.

"That's what we should focus on now. With our mother's thirteen days of mourning over, we need to prioritize our father's health. We may not have our mother anymore, but at least we have our father. I can sense and see our mother within him." Kripa's words were filled with a mixture of determination and longing. Meanwhile, Krisha had finished nursing and was now observing the outside world, fixated on the people, the birds perched on wires, the passing tractors and motorcycles.

Jaya *dai* also joined the conversation while my father-in-law continued to sleep. The effects of the morphine were strong, causing him to sleep until late in the morning. It was a normal response, as the morphine provided enough pain relief for his body to rest and attempt to heal. While complete recovery was unlikely, at least he could find comfort in sleep.

"The doctor assures us that we should not worry, as this is a side effect of the medication. We can only do our best. We have no control over the situation. Whatever we do, we must approach it with confidence and handle things effectively. Worrying will only hinder our efforts," I explained, glancing at Suman *didi*, whose face appeared flushed and anxious.

Jaya *dai* chimed in, agreeing and absentmindedly picking his nose. Kripa asked for more information on the nature of their father's illness. Suman *didi* perked up, curious about Kripa's inquiry.

"The doctor mentioned that your father has a wound in his digestive system," I responded, lacking the courage to reveal the whole truth. "Dr. Karna wants to see the patient."

Internally, I made a silent promise not to divulge anything until I had taken my father-in-law to the doctor once more, buying myself some time to figure out how to break the news gently.

"In that case, both you and Kripa can take our father to the doctor. We will take care of the house," Suman *didi* offered, looking at me for confirmation.

We all agreed to this arrangement.

Later in the afternoon, I confided in Jaya *dai*, sharing my plan to disclose the father's illness once we reached Kathmandu, where I would find a suitable moment to break the news to Kripa. Jaya *dai* found the idea agreeable.

The main decision of the day was that Kripa and I would take my father-in-law to see Dr. Ambuj Karna in two days' time.

As the impending task of sharing the truth about their father's illness loomed over me, I felt a whirlwind of emotions encircle me. Anxiety gripped my heart as I grappled with the fear of how Kripa and Suman *didi* would react to the news. The weight of responsibility pressed down on me, heavy and inescapable. Uncertainty and unease intertwined as I promised myself to delay the revelation until after the doctor's visit, hoping to gather strength and find the most compassionate approach. The path ahead seemed daunting, but a flicker of determination ignited within me, driven by the desire to support my family through this journey.

Chapter Sixteen

Declaration of God's Death

December 16, 2019

Breakfast was a leisurely affair, and we left for Kathmandu around eight in the morning. We had booked tickets over the phone the day before on a tourist bus with high reviews for its comfortable seats, on-time arrivals, and careful driving. We opted for a bus since a flight might be canceled due to fog; plus, we were happy to avoid the risk of a plane crash in the high hills and mountains. Krisha also would feel more comfortable in the tourist bus than in a cramped and bumpy microbus, where she might get motion sick.

"What do you think, *Budho*?" Kripa kept saying in a sentimental tone. "Do you think he will recover?"

Her focus was more on the health of her father than Krisha on her lap. To lighten the mood and provide some comfort, I attempted to inject a touch of humor by repeating my joke.

"Perhaps we should indulge in a bottle of whisky and some venison once we reach Kathmandu, what do you think, father?"

A smile graced my *sasuraba's* lips, stirring something that looked like strength returning, while his eyes radiated a quiet joy.

The monotonousness of the bus ride lulled Krisha to sleep, and she lay on our laps for most of the trip. I felt relieved to be back with Kripa and Krisha by my side, and I enjoyed a short respite from my exhaustion and stress. Krisha still considered me a stranger. It was my first chance to spend time with them after coming back from America. I felt content.

We stopped for lunch at Trishuli Riverside Restaurant, which was full of passengers from other buses. The passengers were paying for meals and serving themselves, while others were gazing at the giant hills to the north as they ate or smoked cigarettes over sips of coffee. It felt like a resort. The

Trisuli River flowed beside the restaurant, merging with the Marsyangdi River a few miles away. The scene reminded me of a song: *Trisuli bagera marsyangdima jharechh timro maya lau malai raksi jhai chadhechh* ("Like Trishuli fell into Marsyangdi, your love got on me like alcohol").

However, more than my love of the song, my father-in-law's sickness was making me feel intoxicated with stress. My feelings were compounded by my wife Kripa's own feelings of stress. Pretending that I needed to use the bathroom, I left Kripa and Krisha briefly and went behind the restaurant to smoke a cigarette. I smoked over some sips of coffee, looking toward the hills in the north and the Trishuli River at their feet.

"Shit, life," I whispered. "This beautiful life is so fleeting."

Kripa took out some utensils from her bag and poured some *lito* (porridge) into lukewarm water to feed Krisha. My father-in-law ate some rice with chicken soup. After a half-hour break, we got back onto the bus and the driver started the engine.

By the time we reached Kalanki, it was two in the afternoon. An hour-long taxi ride later, we were finally home in Tikathali. We couldn't go straight to the hospital to see the doctor—we didn't have an appointment.

Despite their sadness and worry, my parents were glad to see us. This was their second meeting with my *sasuraba*. We were still silently mourning the death of Kripa's mother and worried about my father-in-law's health.

After we had dinner, we got our bed ready for Kripa's father. My parents went upstairs to sleep in the prayer room.

Finally, alone with Kripa, I made an attempt to break the news about her father. Krisha had already fallen asleep in bed next to Kripa. It took me a while to decide how to tell Kripa.

"Kripa, we must accept whatever comes in our lives. Everything that happened in those two weeks was so bizarre that one could hardly believe it."

I silently thought if Kripa's father had replaced her mother, we could justify it because her father had an ulcer twenty years ago, and nearly died but by God's grace he survived that surgery although I didn't have clear reasons to justify my thoughts.

I continued. "All of you had lost hope that your father would survive. We must thank God for this. Certain things are not under our control. Despite his health, he continued to drink alcohol and didn't take good care of his body. Because of all this, the doctor says your father has a big wound, but we should not be scared. We should have patience and continue to find options to cure him. Dr. Ambuj has also said it would be good if we can start chemo." I hugged her and stroked her hair.

As soon as Kripa heard me talking about chemo, she startled and said, "What do you mean by chemo? Does my father have cancer?"

"That is what the report shows," I said, watching carefully for Kripa's reaction to the news. I was unable to control my pounding heart, and I feared that Kripa would start sobbing her own heart out. I hugged her when her voice cracked and became muffled.

"I always say that everything happens for a reason. God gave you our daughter, Krisha," I said, looking at Krisha again. "I came into your life, and that made your parents very happy. But your mother has been snatched away from us. That was not under our control. We must change this tragedy into a creative force. Death can come for anyone at any time. Who knows? Tomorrow one of us may lose our lives without any forewarning. Yet we go on, holding steady in the face of life's fragility—trusting that each step still matters. I am with you. You will see your parents in my eyes, in your daughter's eyes. You will see your own life, joy, happiness, your parents' dreams in our eyes. We will see our happiness and dreams in your eyes," I said, kissing her forehead.

"I always thought there was a God, that God existed, but for me God is dead today. My God is dead," Kripa said, sobbing and hiccupping.

To hear Kripa say such a thing was shocking, because she always believed in worshipping the gods and frequently visited temples. She worshipped God every morning and put *tika* on her forehead. I couldn't imagine her declaring the death of God at any other moment. But this time I could hear her desolation. This one time, I could imagine the pain and grief she was going through.

"Since my mother died, God could have helped my father so I could have at least some hope in life. How can I find a way to go on? An evil person doesn't have to endure a life like I am going through right now, and no sinner has to suffer such a tragedy," she said.

I understood her need to vent her emotions of frustrations, anger, pain, and pathos. I continued to wipe her tears and kiss her head.

"I will talk to the doctor tomorrow. Please don't cry. Please stay calm. I can cancel my plans to go to America and stay with you to support the family. Whatever happens, let it happen. There is nothing greater than the happiness of my family. Since there is no guarantee in life, what else should we live for? We don't know what we're doing or where we're heading. Please wait. I will talk to the doctor tomorrow and discuss the efficacy of chemo. It has helped many cancer patients, and many of them have survived," I said.

I massaged her back and tried to lull her. She tried to remain quiet, but looked dejected. She couldn't fall asleep but tossed and turned restlessly.

"Let's not share this with your father yet," I said.

She was okay with that.

Chapter Seventeen

Sightseers

December 17, 2019

I held onto hope that the doctor would uncover potential solutions to alleviate my *sasuraba's* health condition, bringing him a sense of ease. If a complete cure was unattainable, any reduction in his pain would be a blessing. Though they say palliative care focuses on improving the quality of life and easing patient discomfort, the reality is far from easy. Witnessing my *sasuraba* in agony reverberated through the hearts of everyone around him, intensifying our own distress. I held onto the hope that Dr. Karna would discover ways to address these concerns, an ever-present thought occupying my mind.

We lunched earlier than usual and left for Bir Hospital around nine in the morning. I asked my parents to take care of Krisha. Kathmandu was its usual busy and dusty self as we took a bus from Tikathali to Baneswor, then transferred to a microbus that stopped near the hospital. I instructed Kripa and her father to wait in the downstairs area while I checked on Dr. Karna's schedule.

On the fifth floor, a woman in a blue *sari* informed me that Dr. Karna held appointments on Mondays and Wednesdays but could be reached at his private clinic on Tuesdays. She generously handed me his phone number.

I called him immediately and introduced myself, explaining that I was at Bir Hospital with my father-in-law. He arranged for us to meet at four that evening at Alka Hospital in Jaulakhel, and I felt a wave of relief at securing an appointment.

I took the lift down to the first floor where Kripa and her father were waiting for me with hope and sadness in their eyes. I explained about the appointment. We still had six hours to go before the appointment, and we could reach the clinic within half an hour. We had a dilemma as to whether to go back home and come back to see him later, or wait the six hours.

"Let's not go home now. We meet the doctor first and then go home. We could spend some time at the zoo at Jaulakhel. If my father feels able, he could join us," Kripa proposed.

We went straight to the zoo.

We paid two dollars per head and purchased three tickets. The zoo brought back memories of my visit fifteen years ago. The facilities looked the same, but the number of zoo animals in total decreased. At that time, there was no Orangutan, but now he was the star attraction. I found the surrounding area a bit greener and better maintained from outside, but the conditions of the animals remained the same.

Deer, rhinos, tigers, birds, snakes, monkeys, langurs, and peacocks drew the crowds. Visitors watched with delight—pointing, laughing, snapping photos. But no one seemed to notice the quiet misery behind the fences.

The zoo turned innocence into spectacle.

Beneath the cheer and noise, it was clear: this wasn't a sanctuary. It was a stage. The animals weren't being cared for; they were being used—boxed into enclosures, paraded for profit. Their suffering was silent, but everywhere.

I felt deeply unsettled by the gap between their pain and the crowd's joy.

"Krisha would love this," Kripa commented.

My father-in-law cried out "Ouch!" and held his stomach, pressing down on it with both hands. "I cannot walk anymore. You go visit. I will stay here sitting and lying under the trees."

We had purchased some peanuts, so Kripa took them out from her handbag and gave it to her father, saying, "Okay, please eat these. We will come back right away."

Leaving Kripa's father there for a few minutes, we walked around the zoo.

I felt that our pain seemed small next to the quiet misery of those animals. Perhaps the animals endured more pain than my father-in-law. Encroaching on their freedoms, we limited them completely. *What wrong had these animals done to us?* They were penalized and deprived of their rights to live freely and independently.

As I mingled with the crowd of people watching the tiger named Shiva in the zoo, I was reminded of Rainer Maria Rilke's poem *"The Panther"* and *"The Exile"* by British poet Alan Duff. I felt their pain as if I walked in their shoes, silently reciting these lines:

As he paces in cramped circles, over and over, the movement of his powerful soft strides   is like a ritual dance around a center   in which a mighty will stands paralyzed.— from "The Panther" by Rainer Maria Rilke

These days, it was not just the animal rights activists talking about the rights of animals. Yes, animals cannot argue or be logical like human beings, but they also have their own language. They can also feel pain and grief. They care for their families. But who can understand them? At that moment I remembered what the founder of moral philosophy Jeremy Bentham, had said: "The question was not whether they could reason or talk, but could they suffer?"

Bentham's statement felt profoundly true—it applied to all living beings and their right to life and freedom. Every creature can feel pain just as humans do. Animals experience anxiety, frustration, joy, and the bonds of family. The animals in this zoo must be living a life of silent ache. I thought of an old Nepali song sung by Manik Ratna: *ma pani ta manis hu mero pani mutu dukhchh/malai pani timlai jastai hasna, runa man lagchh*—I too am human, my heart aches too; I also long to laugh and cry, just like you."

As I strolled through the zoo, I couldn't help but imagine myself in the animals' place, sensing that each one carried its own story, its own unheard song. That feeling reminded me of E. B. White's beloved book, *Charlotte's Web*, where animals form deep emotional connections with a young girl. Her love for a pig, and her efforts to save him from slaughter, left a lasting impression on me. I decided then that one day, I would share that story with Krisha—perhaps read it aloud in Nepali—so its message of compassion and kinship would speak to her, too.

In the middle of the zoo, there was a pool—calm and quiet. Ducks were swimming, dunking their heads in and out. There were some boats in the shape of a duck, and visitors sailed along in the pond, enjoying the greenery. The landscape was filled with long green Sal trees that stood like yogis in meditation.

"*Buwa* is waiting for us alone; he might have stomach pain. Let's go," Kripa said. She was holding my hand while in the other she grasped a bag of peanuts.

"Sure," I said, and we rushed back to where he was sitting.

My father-in-law was slumbering, leaning against the tree, and we let him rest. We sat nearby, eating peanuts. Some pigeons flew and came near us and started picking the peanut shells we had thrown nearby. Kripa gave them some more, and the pigeons flocked around. They were not afraid of us now. We became their friends right away. *There is no enemy in this world, and as such, we must know how to make them our friends*, I thought. We had earned the trust of those pigeons, so they were flocking without any fear and picking up the peanuts right in front of us. It was nearly four o'clock.

"Perhaps we should go to the hospital," I said as I got up from the ground. "We can wait for the doctor there. In the meantime, we can purchase a prescription ticket. Maybe your father is hungry—we could get something to eat at the cafeteria."

We headed to the hospital, which wasn't far. We reached it in ten minutes. Kripa bought the prescription ticket for five dollars. We still had fifteen minutes before the scheduled appointment time. In the cafeteria, we had some samosas and tea. My sasuraba didn't have an appetite and only sipped a sugar-free tea.

The doctor hadn't arrived by four thirty. I finally texted him: "We are still waiting for you. My one-year-old daughter is at home. Her mother, who needs to breastfeed her, is also with me, waiting for you."

The doctor replied immediately: "I am on the way. A bit late due to traffic jam."

Kripa phoned my parents and asked about Krisha—what she ate, or if she had eaten lito. After another thirty minutes, Dr. Karna arrived, looking apologetic for his lateness, though he didn't say "sorry," a gesture that was simply taken for granted. I greeted him with a "Namaste." We all entered his office for the appointment.

Dr. Karna asked my father-in-law to lie down on the bed and pressed on his belly for a few moments before inviting him to sit in a nearby chair. With a kind smile, the doctor encouraged him to express any concerns. My father-in-law, however, only mentioned his pressing pain and requested medication to alleviate it, repeating his need for pain relief when prompted again.

Not wanting to delve further into chemotherapy discussions in front of him, I gestured for Kripa to take her father outside. Once alone, I expressed my desire for him to start chemotherapy, acknowledging that while it might not cure him, it could extend his life.

Dr. Karna agreed but reminded me that the decision was ultimately ours. I shared my concern that the family wasn't ready for chemotherapy yet and that my father-in-law remained unaware of his condition.

"I think your father-in-law already knows what he has. What do you think? Do you think that he doesn't suspect anything when you are talking to me in private? He must have already sensed his disease. Perhaps he thinks that you are stressed out, and he might be pretending he has no idea. That is what I am thinking," Dr. Karna said, trying to be reasonable and sensible. He seemed to be urging me out of his office, closing drawers and collecting papers on the table.

"You might be right," I said. "Okay, I will try to talk to my wife too about this, and I will come see you again. We are very thankful to you for your advice, time, and how you behaved so humbly." Dr. Karna added a few more morphine tablets and syrup to the prescription. We stamped the prescription slip and went to another pharmacy where we could purchase the medicine. It was already six o'clock, and the sun had sunk beneath the horizon. The days were shorter in the Winter.

"Krisha might be hungry and looking for me. My breasts are filled with milk, and I am feeling uneasy," Kripa said.

I called my father over the phone and asked about her.

"Where are you now? She fell asleep hungry while crying and saying, 'Mommy, mommy.' She didn't even eat *lito*. Come soon," my father said, urging us to return.

Listening to my father's words made me feel terrible, as if my heart had broken into pieces. My one-year-old daughter had fallen asleep crying "mommy" and didn't eat anything.

"Poor Krisha!" I whispered. "She is also destined to suffer due to this. Our fate. Her fate." I didn't mention this to Kripa, as it would only sadden her more. I said, "Krisha is fine."

By the time we got home, it was nine o'clock. Krisha was already asleep. After twelve long hours apart, I finally saw her face—still and soft in the glow of the bedside light. Her tiny lips were dry and slightly puckered, perhaps from missing her mother's milk. I watched her breathe, steady and unaware, and swallowed hard.

I couldn't bring myself to eat. After murmuring good night to the others, I lay down in the living room, aching with exhaustion. *Tomorrow*, I told myself. *Tomorrow had to be better.*

Chapter Eighteen

When Mountain Becomes Flute

December 18, 2019

"*Jwaisaap*, the doctor has given me enough medicine for now. If I must come back, I will come. It's not that far from Pokhara to Kathmandu—about 200 kilometers. Let me go now," my *sasuraba* said, as if traveling to Pokhara would make him feel better.

"Why do you want to go so early? You don't have anything to do there, either. You can stay with us. Please treat this as your home. You won't miss anything. If you must see the doctor again, you'd have to come all the way from Pokhara," I said, trying to grab a remote and turn the TV on.

"If my father wants to go, let him go. He has his friends there. He can kill time by playing cards with them. He feels a lot better in his own house. We can send him on the plane, and Suman *didi* will come pick him up at the airport. What do you think, *Budho*?" Kripa said, looking at me and trying to see things from her father's perspective.

I decided Kripa was right, so I used an eswea app on the phone to purchase the plane ticket online. The earliest available ticket was at noon.

Kripa made lunch and served all of us. My father-in-law bid my parents farewell, with the hope of seeing them for the next doctor's appointment. Krisha waived her hands, gesturing "goodbye" to her grandfather, and cried because he was leaving her. Kripa and I went to the airport to drop him off.

We told Suman *didi* to pick him up at the airport. My *sasuraba* entered security with the ticket in his hand. Kripa watched him with longing until he disappeared in the line. My father-in-law's eyes were completely sunken, and his big body had turned, figuratively speaking, into a thin flute. His walk lacked enthusiasm and all his energy was gone.

"My father has changed so quickly. He was big as a mountain. This body is not his," she said, with tears brimmed up in her eyes.

My sadness intensified at her words, but I choked the emotion down. "What can we do, *Budhi*? The disease is cruel," I said, drawing her closer to my chest while air passengers walked here and there, dragging their luggage. "Whatever has to happen will happen. We need to accept that. If grieving cannot make things better, there is no point in crying. The best thing we can do is to try to find the right treatment. That's it."

"Perhaps he is also in pain from losing his wife," Kripa said.

"Of course," I said. "They spent many years together, and your mother was the one to take full care of your father. He must now miss her more than ever." It was a truth that no one could deny, since he himself had expressed that loss in a conversation I'd had with him earlier.

"God has been really cruel to us. If God wanted someone's life, why didn't He choose someone who had already lived most of his life or had seen the whole world or who is awaiting death or who is in a coma and has to spend all his life in bed?" she said, venting her frustration and anger.

"How can everything be exactly the way we think, *Budhi*?" I said, trying to comfort her. "I think everything has a reason. Perhaps God was looking for a good human being. Perhaps he needs a nice person up in Heaven." I rubbed her back tenderly and said, "Let's go home. Now your father will be back home soon. Krisha must be missing you. She hasn't seen enough of us. We also must give her our time."

Krisha was playing with her grandparents. I also held her in my arms, looking at her eyes and teasing her. I had to be closer to her. I had to make sure that she would know me as her father. I decided to spend all my time with Krisha that day, trying to gain her trust. Kripa took some rest in bed saying, "Krisha woke up at five o'clock and started crying. Perhaps she had a bad dream. She complained and grunted the whole night and wouldn't let me get much sleep."

"It is not easy to be a mother," I said, and I thought that this was perhaps how Kripa's mother had raised her as well. But her mother was dead. I believed we could never receive more love than we received from our own mothers.

I thought about a parent's role in shaping a child's life. The *Bhagvat Gita* says a child's character—whether noble like Gokarna or wayward like Dhandukari—depends more on the mother, who stays closest in those early years.

What kind of person will Krisha become?

I hadn't been there for her. Not really. And that thought stayed with me, heavier than scripture.

Chapter Nineteen

Prisoner of Indecisiveness on Depression Day

December 26, 2019

After sending my *sasuraba* back to Pokhara, we spent another full week with my family. Knowing about her father's disease, Kripa spent every day with tears in her eyes. However, Krisha was there to remind her of the other joyous part of life. Krisha had also started speaking a few words like *mamu*, meaning mother. The word, spoken so innocently, brightened my wife's face as she hugged our daughter.

In Pokhara, in the meantime, Suman *didi* took care of her father at his house in Sisuwa. The decision was made to share the care of their father by taking turns—two weeks by Suman *didi* and another two weeks by Kripa, meaning Kripa had to return to Pokhara. Suman *didi* also had her own business matters to attend to, and she had to care for her kids, send them to school, and do other household chores. No matter what, one had to move on and continue with life. In Nepali society, a mother's responsibility is much more burdensome than that of fathers.

Suman *didi* video called Kripa. Her face was somber, she was sneezing and coughing, and her eyes looked ruddy from lack of sleep.

"With mother gone and father in a fragile condition, I am really scared, Kripa. His morphine is also running out. If possible, please come to Pokhara soon, and don't forget to bring more morphine tablets."

"Oh no, what happened to him? He was okay the other day," she said with her voice trembling. She looked away from the phone to distract herself. "How can we make him feel better?"

"I don't know, Kripa. I wish you were here with me so we could support each other," Suman *didi* said, sulking.

Kripa hung up the phone and immediately turned to me. "*Budho*, what can we do now? Your time to return to America is coming soon as well. I am already worried. How can I be happy without you around?" Kripa said, sniffling back tears.

I looked into her eyes, seeing helplessness, as if she had nobody there to trust and support and love except for me. Her eyes filled with anxious anticipation. If I didn't support her, she would shatter into a million pieces.

I still had fifteen more days before returning to America. After that, my spring semester would begin, and I had to be on campus to teach in-person classes. I had found that position with much effort and had only started it four months before. I couldn't give it up, as I knew many other people would be willing to make huge sacrifices to obtain that job. It was a great accomplishment on my part after finishing my Ph.D.

I struggled to address her concerns. I cleared my throat, hoping to find an answer. "I know you will feel forlorn without me," I said.

I looked into Kripa's eyes. I caressed her face, pushing a strand of hair in place by the side of her ear. "Or should I give up? What do you think? Should I leave Amerika-Shamerika and the job too? Life is so short, and nobody knows what might happen."

She remained silent. One side of my brain said there was nothing more important than the presence and support of family. I should be with them so I could support Kripa and work together with her. The other side of my brain said I must go. I had already spent twelve years in America. Right now, I could help out by living in Nepal with my own family. But the responsibilities on my shoulders were growing by the day after the birth of Krisha. The family would have major expectations of me, and I had to fulfill them.

I looked at Krisha. She was growing up like a bamboo shoot. She had just started saying *mamu* in her little toddler voice. If I could take her to America and give her a quality education there, she would thank me for her bright future. People across the world would die to go to America, the country of their dreams. Hardly any could obtain a visa. I also remembered my difficulty when I got my visa. How hard those days were, and when I finally did receive the visa, tears of joy had rolled down my cheeks. Now I also had a job at an American university, and there was no way I would ever make that much money in Nepal. I still had a fifty-thousand-dollar student loan to pay back in America, and I could not pay that with a salaried job in Nepal. I had to make more money to fulfill my wife and daughter's needs. I mulled over all these thoughts as they gushed out like water.

Kripa finally found her voice. "If you give up the idea of returning to America, I am fine. I lost all my joy and happiness and desire with the death of my mother. My desire to go abroad is gone. I have no hope left in my life. If my husband is not around, I will feel abandoned."

She leaned against my shoulder and sniffled again. Her words rang true to me, but the thoughts were not practical as they were mostly guided by her flood of emotions. Sometimes these emotions have a way of covering the truth, and they can cause people to make quick decisions that turn out to be incorrect. Still, I respected her emotions, and I felt the same emotions welling up in me. I wanted to go with her flow, to consider giving up on America, but I had to force myself to be rational, I had to think practically. I remembered a line from *Bhagavat Gita*: "Don't decide when you are in pain and only guided by a fit of emotions."

"Do you really think I can give up on America, *Budhi*?" I asked Kripa again to confirm what she had said earlier.

Krisha was playing on the bed and throwing her feet up in the air.

"I'm not sure how to answer your question. I cannot say 'yes,' nor can I say 'no.' Isn't there a way you can teach another four more months from here, *Budho*?" she asked.

Her proposal actually made sense, though I wasn't sure whether I would be allowed to do it. I didn't have the right answer for her immediately. There might be some possibility, however, because I had previously taught classes online. I would have to ask the administration about it. I really liked Kripa's proposal. I thought I didn't always need to agree with my partner all the time, but when I am in a state of indecisiveness and my partner offers a sensible alternative that guides me, she is a good partner. I believe we need a good partner in such difficult times. I started thinking about how to make Kripa's proposal work.

"This sounds like a good idea, *Budhi*. I think I should write an email to my boss about it," I said in joy, clapping my hands at the idea. "I will write a letter today and I hope she will reply to me by tomorrow."

"Okay then, you do that first, *Budho*, and after lunch we can go see the doctor. I think we can meet Dr. Ambuj Karna because today he is scheduled at Bir Hospital," Kripa said, standing up, sneezing and clearing her nose using a handkerchief. She went over to the closet to choose her clothes for the day. I nodded in approval, then went to my laptop in the library and began composing the email. After reading through it twice, I hit the send button.

I played with Krisha on the laptop, showing her toddler videos and pictures of animals while Kripa cooked a meal in the kitchen.

After lunch, we were ready to leave for the hospital.

"Mom, we have to go see the doctor at the hospital in Pokhara tomorrow, to buy more medicine for Kripa's father."

My mother was in the living room lying on the couch.

"Krisha, Kripa, and I are going back," I said.

"Oh, tomorrow, really?" My mother's voice was heavy, as if she had received terrible news. "Do you have to go? If Krisha were three or four years old, you could leave her with us, but now she would be looking for her mother's milk."

We met Dr. Karna at the hospital and informed him about the family not being ready for chemo and asked him for the prescription of more morphine medicine.

"As you wish, Mr. Tulasi. If your *sasuraba* wants chemo, it would be better to do so sooner rather than later. Since I am your doctor, I am giving you my best recommendation, but it is all up to you," Dr. Karna said with his soft voice while writing the prescription on a piece of paper.

"Dr. Saap, can you please prescribe at least a month's worth? We will not be coming back until next month as we are going to Pokhara." My words might have given the doctor the impression that we preferred morphine over Chemo.

"Sorry! We are not allowed to prescribe it for more than fifteen days. You can buy more in Pokhara if needed," he suggested.

I thanked Dr. Karna, got the prescription stamped, and headed to the hospital pharmacy. On the way home, we picked up a kilo of avocados from a fruit stand in New Baneswor—crowded with buses, cars, and motorbikes weaving through pedestrians at the intersection.

We'd take the fruit to Pokhara for *Sasuraba*. Kripa was always thinking of what her father could eat to feel stronger. It had become her quiet mission.

When we got home, Krisha was crying and saying, "*mamu, mamu.*"

"Krisha drank a little bit of water, but no milk," my mother said. At least Kripa had fed her a little bit of porridge before we left. As soon as she saw Kripa, she jumped into her mother's lap and latched her mouth to her mother's breast, holding on for dear life. The sun was already setting by five o'clock. Krisha fell asleep while sucking her mother's milk, without eating any *lito*.

"That's okay. I will breastfeed her if she wakes," Kripa said, showering Krisha with her motherly love. After dinner, we also went to bed so we could get up early to leave for Pokhara. Kripa had already packed all our belongings and her daughter's paraphernalia into a small suitcase.

"Darling, don't you miss me?" I expressed in a tender tone, realizing it had been quite some time since we'd had the chance to delve into each other's emotions, ever since I'd returned from America. Drawing her closer, I showered her with kisses, cherishing our connection.

"Of course, I do," she replied, holding me tightly in her embrace. "But you know my mind is consumed by my father's illness."

"I completely understand, and that's precisely why I am here with you," I assured her, gently unbuttoning her clothing and resting my head upon her chest, peppering her with more kisses. A surge of electricity coursed through her, and her breath quickened. I held her tightly, conveying how much I had missed her. "When was the last time we were together like this? Can you recall?"

A smile, which had been somewhat elusive, graced her lips, comforting me greatly.

"Now you're being naughty," she teased, turning her face away playfully.

"We must remember that everything follows its own course, and fretting over it won't change a thing. Let's focus on each other this once, my love," I encouraged, and hoped she would let herself be present with me. Eventually we extinguished the lights, finding love and peace in each other's presence.

Chapter Twenty

Whistle of a Riddled Heart

December 27, 2019

In the midst of the pouring rain and the ever-changing weather in Kathmandu, we hurriedly made our way to Kalanki station. I held Krisha tightly against my chest, shielding her from the rain as we frantically searched for shelter. It pained me to see her discomfort, but I was relieved that she remained dry, even as I myself became drenched and shivered from the cold.

Finally reaching the station, we secured our tickets to Pokhara and boarded the micro bus, seeking refuge from the elements. A call from my father interrupted the bustling atmosphere, his hoarse voice expressing concern. "Where are you now?" he asked.

"We are on the bus," I replied, ensuring him of our safety and his grandchild's well-being. After a brief exchange, he bid us farewell. Krisha had drifted off to sleep, her tiny body still pressed against mine like a warm little kitten. Kripa tenderly wrapped a small blanket around her, her damp hair dripping like a melting candle. I couldn't help but question why our young daughter had to endure all the challenges of these journeys, especially the bouts of vomiting along winding roads. Nevertheless, we eventually arrived home.

Upon reaching Kripa's home, we were greeted by the sight of Suman *didi*, Zenith, Araju, and my *sasuraba* basking in the fading rays of the westward-sinking sun. Their warm welcomes filled the air as they waved from the veranda. Kripa's eyes welled with tears as she entered the house, the silence and those hanging pictures reminded her of everything that was gone. She wiped her watery eyes with the side of her T-shirt and struggled to find comfort in the familiar surroundings.

Krisha, recognizing her grandfather, exclaimed with joy, "Baa, baa!" Her spirits lifted, and she was happy to play with him. Meanwhile, I inquired about my father-in-law's health, and he shared his ongoing struggles. Despite some relief with an increase in the dosage of morphine, his body still felt uneasy, plagued by pain. Although he seemed somewhat better during our video chats, witnessing him in person only reinforced the extent of his suffering. His sunken eyes and skeletal appearance spoke volumes.

The entire family's focus had now shifted toward my *sasuraba* and his health, partly replacing thoughts of my *Sasuma*. We stood united, dedicated to his treatment and harboring hope for his survival. When asked about Jaya *dai*, Suman *didi* informed us that he was at the store but would be joining us later that night.

As evening descended, Jaya *dai* returned, and we gathered around for a shared dinner. I administered the prescribed dose of morphine to my father-in-law, his weariness causing him to doze off on the couch while we watched television.

Observing him in that moment, a poem by the 20th-century American poet Ezra Pound, *In a Station of the Metro*, echoed in my mind:

"The apparition of these faces in the crowd; Petals on a wet, black bough."

A sense of transience and beauty permeated the air, reminding me of the fragility of life and the delicate balance we sought to maintain in the face of uncertainty. Together, we braced ourselves for the challenges ahead, cherishing the fleeting moments of togetherness and nurturing the flicker of hope that remained.

Chapter Twenty-One

Email, Dipang Lake, and Cards

December 28, 2019

"Did they reply to your email?" Kripa asked me the next morning. We all were still lying in bed, not fully awake. My father-in-law was snoring. I got up and started stretching my body. Kripa was referring to the email I had sent to Jennifer, my boss, regarding the possibility of teaching online in the spring.

"Not yet," I said, yawning. "I emailed her just yesterday. They usually don't bother to check their emails on Friday, or on the weekend. The office reopens on Monday, and then I am sure they will check their emails. I have done my job on my side. The rest is in their hands."

"What did you write in the email?" Kripa asked, trying to make sure I had worded it nicely. Her inquiries brought out the journalist in her.

"Why do you need all the details?" I asked, picking up my Samsung phone and scrolling down to find the email I had written to my boss. "Here you go."

Dear Jennifer,

I am writing this email with a heavy heart. I hope we will be able to figure something out. My wife is currently mourning the untimely demise of her mother. She spent time in seclusion for thirteen days, eating unsalted food just once a day. Since we have a twelve-month-old daughter, she also needed to breastfeed. My wife is heartbroken at this unexpected loss, and the bond between her and her mother was incredibly close. My wife has felt forlorn and deserted. Her father has been quite ill, but her mother appeared healthy and young.

Currently, her father has been diagnosed with end-stage pancreatic cancer, and treatment does not appear to be an option. I am handling all of this since my wife has no brother in her family. I think my wife will also lose her father very soon. It has become my duty to handle all of his hospital visits and take care of the family and my daughter. It will be difficult for me and my wife to be separated from each other during this time of unexpected challenges. I do not know what to say to you now. I do not know how to ask you for a favor while you have already done more than what I could imagine.

I am wondering if you could offer me online classes this semester—Spring 2020. I would feel very fortunate and blessed from you. Regarding the courses that require partial meetings, I could meet my students via Skype and video calls from here. In the meantime, I would also continue creating the courses as I have been doing. I am extremely sorry to bring this proposal to you. I know how tough it may cause things on your part, and I feel terrible for undoing all your plans for the semester. This was unexpected, unthinkable, never something we imagined nor wanted. Please advise. I will still try my best to make it to the college for Spring 2020, although the chances seem slim.

Kind regards,
Tulasi Acharya, Ph.D.
Assistant Professor of English

I hoped Jennifer would support my plan to teach online from Nepal. I was keeping my fingers crossed.

If not, I told myself, I could stay. I didn't *have* to go back to America.

But the thought terrified me.

Losing my job would mean more than a paycheck. It would threaten everything—Krisha's future, our only income, the sense of stability my family clung to. As the sole provider, I couldn't afford that risk.

Kripa read the email silently and said, "It was indeed a nice email. I hope they will work on it and let you teach the classes online this coming semester."

"I hope so," I said, moving toward the bathroom. "Let's get up and make some tea?"

***

In the afternoon, Jaya *dai* and I went out after lunch. He drove his motorcycle, and we went further north to the hills that surround Dipang Lake, one of the seven lakes in Pokhara. On the way, I purchased a Surya cigarette and two small cartons of mango juice, one for me and another for Jaya *dai*.

Dipang Lake is not as big as other lakes in Pokhara, such as Fewa or Begnas, but it was serene and scenic. Due to the lack of proper conservation, the water level in the lake was diminishing, and shrubs had started encroaching on the space. It looked like a courtyard of water for the hills that surrounded it. Behind the hills were Mount Annapurna and Dhaulagiri, with a smile that fully bloomed as soon as the purdah of cloud was lifted. The day became clearer. We sat near the shadow which the hills made over the lake and started sipping our mango juice through straws. I lit my cigarette and took a puff with each sip.

"You know, *dai*, our father-in-law's disease can't be cured, and it just feels like he is waiting for death. But when?" I pulled on the cigarette deeply, puffing out, and watching the smoke disperse in all directions.

"This is bizarre, Tulasi. Our s*asuraba* will probably not survive this year, the same year our *sasuma* died. This is very rare," Jaya *dai* said, sipping the juice from the straw and then taking the straw out of the carton.

"You are correct," I said.

I tossed a pebble into the serene lake and watched as it created a series of ripples, gradually expanding and moving away.

"*Sasuraba* drank a lot of alcohol, Tulasi, and without enough food to go with it. Our local alcohol is very strong. He should have paid attention to his health," Jaya *dai* said. "He could have at least had a proper meal and snacks with it."

"That's true, *dai*. He could have done that."

"On top of that, he already had an ulcer twenty years ago when he almost lost his life. It was a prime opportunity for him to learn. After his surgery, he could have quit drinking completely. What can we do now? It is too late now." Jaya *dai* continued recounting information I already knew.

"Perhaps this is what was meant to happen, *dai*," I said. "Not only is our father-in-law suffering from this pain, but so are his daughters, and we are sharing their pain."

"What a scary disease this cancer is! There is no treatment, nor proper medicine. When one has cancer, he dies for sure?" Jaya *dai* wondered.

I was not an expert or specialist about cancer, but based on what I had heard, I responded, "Cancers are very complex, and there are different stages. If it was a first stage, there might be some chance for the patient to survive, but when the person reaches the last stage, it seems he will die for sure. But sometimes this is not true. People with stage one can die, and people with stage four can overcome it. It's very unpredictable." I turned to Jaya *dai*, saying, "Would you smoke the very last pop?"

"Sure. Let me also smoke the last bit of this *jatho* cigarette. I don't see the point of living life sometimes," he said, swearing. He reached out for my cigarette and smoked the last puff, throwing away the butt. We shared our pain and anguish along with the mango juice and the cigarette. The smoke moved out across Dipang Lake.

"There is no point in being stressed out, *dai*. Whatever happens, happens. We can just wish for the best and hope he will not have much pain and that he will live a painless life until he dies," I said, perhaps sounding rude in my honesty.

"That's right," Jaya *dai* agreed. "*Buwa* had plenty of fun in his life before this, but unfortunately, the cancer caught up to him. Life is uncertain."

"Perhaps God balances things out. Our mother-in-law worked hard, managing the household chores and feeding and supporting her husband. That may be the reason for her easy death—she died the minute she collapsed on the road. Perhaps our father-in-law had enough fun already, so now he also has to experience pain. But this pain is a bit unbearable," I said. "I don't have any complaints now. My wish is only for his daughters not to have trauma if he doesn't die quickly." I could think of nothing more to say. I looked into the distance where the hills were standing tall and magnificent.

Jaya *dai* kicked the motorcycle and got it started. I rode behind him, and we went back to the house in Sisuwa. He dropped me off, saying, "I will go to the store for a few hours and be back. What can we do? My business is the only thing I can manage, Tulasi. Life must continue, no matter what." I nodded in agreement.

I went upstairs and found my father-in-law sitting on the verandah, his face etched with pain and one hand pressed against his stomach. The morning sun bathed the space in warmth, yet it seemed powerless to uplift his spirits.

I asked if he was still in pain, fully aware that cancer had only deepened his suffering. He responded with a wince, shifting slightly in his seat. Reflecting on better days, he shared how he had dreamed of spending joyful moments with me, lamenting how his health had thwarted those hopes. His eyes drifted as he recalled his youth, filled with strength and enthusiasm.

Occasionally, he stretched his body and chewed on some tobacco, a familiar ritual that offered him a fleeting distraction from his discomfort. After sipping some water, he gathered his thoughts to continue his story.

He reminisced about moving to Sisuwa and starting a tea stand in the very spot where he built his home. Back then, the city felt like a village, but as more people arrived, businesses began to flourish. Their tea stand was the only one around, drawing in customers, while his wife skillfully managed everything and cared for the children. He never engaged in kitchen chores.

His voice softened with nostalgia as he spoke of how they eventually expanded their tea stand into a restaurant. Evenings buzzed with life, filled with patrons who came to drink but never caused trouble. Those days, he said, were filled with excitement, and the profits from their tea stand had enabled them to buy the house he lived in now.

His eyes sparkled with memories as he spoke. "Our luck began the moment we opened the tea stand," he said, his eyes reflecting memories both sweet and bitter. "Hard work alone isn't enough if luck isn't on your side. I learned that the hard way."

He sighed, the weight of past losses heavy in his voice.

"Before all this, I had two buses running from Pokhara to New Delhi. Everything was going great. I bought land in the city center. But one day, one of the buses had an accident—more than ten passengers died. The insurance payout was substantial, and that's when my bad luck began. I had to sell everything, including the land and the bus, and we became squatters."

His voice grew somber. "We didn't have anything to eat or proper clothing. So, I moved my family to Kathmandu, selling readymade clothes on the street. I carried them around, asking pedestrians to buy them while my wife took care of Suman and Kripa in a rented room. That business didn't support us either, but the tea stand eventually brought back our good fortune."

The warmth of the sun seemed to flicker as he recounted his story. "Once we opened the tea stand, we never lacked money or food—goat meat and chicken became staples, once considered luxuries. People came for the meals. 'Very delicious,' they would say. 'Your wife Gita makes it tasty.' I had to keep a live goat or two ready every day. I had so much energy back then; I could go out, kill a goat, butcher it, and prepare it for cooking—all within an hour. Customers were always surprised."

He leaned back, pride evident in his voice.

"Everyone in the area knew me. If you mentioned my name, they praised me. I've never taken money for free; many borrowed from me and never returned it. I'm content with that. Money is meaningless. I had it, lost it all, and still managed to build this house. So please, don't brag about money. It's just a means, not the end."

He continued to narrate his past to me, his days of hardship in the hotel, about which Kripa had already told me when I first fell in love with her. I felt his life story was more authentic and credible when I heard it from his own mouth. While my s*asuraba* shared his tale, I found myself visualizing the story Kripa had recounted earlier. It was through the exchanged stories of our parents' struggles and perseverance that our love for each other blossomed. Our hearts intertwined as we listened, sharing our deepest emotions and forging a profound connection based on common experiences and bonds.

In the meantime, a few neighbors visited and said, "Resham, would you like to play cards?"

Almost every day, his friends came to play cards in a room on the second floor. He spent some time watching others play when he didn't feel up to it.

"I cannot play, but I can watch you playing," he said as he went into the room downstairs. I sat in the living room. Krisha was napping after her lunch. I looked at her and wished I could pick her up and hold her close to my chest. Kripa was washing clothes at the tap outside. Suman *didi* was cleaning the kitchen.

We all gathered again back on the veranda.

"Kripa, since you are here, we'd like to go into Pokhara. We also have to open the store. In two weeks, Zenith will need to take his exams. So, we will come back after his exams, and you can go back to Kathmandu," Suman *didi* said.

"That's fine," Kripa said, and I agreed with her. Since my father-in-law didn't have a son, it was his daughters' duty to take care of him.

Suman *didi* and her family left Sisuwa for Pokhara bazaar, saying they would come back in two weeks. The house felt lonelier and more accursed. Deep down, I was aware that this moment would eventually arrive, when each one of us would have to depart, one by one, following our individual paths.

Chapter Twenty-Two

The Light of a Lamp About to Die

December 29, 2019

Sisuwa, with its cold climate, experiences frequent fog during winter, often obstructing the view of the snow-covered *Machhapuchhre* and *Annapurna* mountains to the north until later in the day. The sun struggles to break through the dense fog, creating an ethereal atmosphere. Nature, like life itself, is ever-changing, and that is its inherent beauty. Just as seasons transition, happiness and sadness, life and death, health and sickness are intertwined like the two sides of a constantly shifting coin. To live a meaningful life, we must adapt to these changes. We must recognize that control is an illusion, and instead we must embrace the flow of time and the shifting nature of our surroundings, as they influence us and the world around us.

When I returned from the bathroom, my father-in-law suddenly started screaming in pain and holding his belly. "I am in pain, *aiya*! I am dying." I opened the morphine syrup right away and gave him some to drink. Even after ten minutes, his pain wasn't abating. He started shrieking even louder.

"My father would not cry out in this much pain unless he was truly dying. We need to bring him to the hospital," Kripa said, rushing out of bed in fear, her hair disheveled. "Please call an ambulance. Let's bring him to the hospital." Her voice was frantic. Krisha also woke up and started crying upon seeing her mother.

"Please, be calm" I told Kripa.

I called an ambulance, which brought him to the nearby hospital—Lekhnath Community Lions Hospital. He was admitted there. As soon as we reached the hospital, the doctor gave him an injection of a painkiller, and he felt immediate relief. I also called Suman *didi* and Jaya *dai*. They arrived at the hospital in half an hour after closing up their store.

The nurses checked his blood sugar level.

"It is extremely high at 600. Is he taking his diabetes medication and insulin?" the nurse asked.

"It's been three days since I've taken insulin," my father-in-law answered weakly.

We had told him to stop using the insulin when he lost his appetite completely. We thought the insulin might be the reason for his loss of appetite. We thought we were smarter than the doctors. I realized then that we should never have gone against the doctors' orders.

"No, you must continue the insulin," the nurse said.

After my father-in-law felt some relief, we asked the nurse if we could go back home.

"Wait until Dr. Prakash comes this afternoon. We should follow what he says," the nurse said.

My father-in-law's cousins also came to visit him at the hospital. They looked frightened.

The doctors and nurses kept saying, "Please do not gather around the patient's bed."

Despite the nurses' repeated warnings, no one listened. Visitors crowded around the bed—one perched at the foot, another squeezed in at the side, the rest stood close and chatted like it was a family picnic. The ward buzzed with noise and movement, rules forgotten.

In America, only one person visited the patient at a time—it is very systematic, and people obey the rules.

There were many beds in the ward. Some patients were on oxygen. Others cried out, "I'm dying," their voices rising above the chaos.

I felt helpless seeing all the patients struggling with their various diseases. Kripa was holding Krisha and looking at her father.

"Krisha might be hungry," I told Kripa and Suman *didi*. "You both can go home. The kids are hungry. Jaya *dai* and I will stay here." Kripa and Suman *didi* left for home, which was just fifteen minutes away from the hospital.

In the afternoon, Kripa's cousin Meenu Sister came to the hospital with lunch. She lived at Begnastal, a twenty-minute walk east from the hospital, which was between Sisuwa Chowk and Begnas lake. I realized why relatives were so important during a tragedy.

Dr. Prakash had not arrived by one thirty. Jaya dai was on his phone, sitting beside my father-in-law's bed. I spent some time chatting with other patients and asking about the causes and symptoms of their diseases.

Kripa called me. "Did Dr. Prakash arrive?"

"Not yet," I said. "Might be on the way."

"I am trying to put Krisha to bed for a nap. How is my father now?"

"He is a lot better now. Don't worry," I said and hung up the phone.

Soon after, Dr. Prakash arrived. Short and nearly bald with sloped shoulders, he looked to be in his late thirties. He had no idea of my father-in-law's medical history, and I couldn't explain to him about the cancer in front of the patient. I worried that if I showed him all the reports right in front of my father-in-law, he might learn about his disease and feel even more hopeless. It might shorten his longevity. So, I requested to speak with Dr. Prakash in his office, bringing out all the reports to show him. "We have not told the patient about his disease."

"This is serious. We have no way to cure it. We can try chemo or continue with the morphine," Dr. Prakash said, echoing what the other doctors had told us. "End-stage pancreatic cancer is extremely serious."

"It is really sad, Doctor," I said. "What should we do? Can we take him home now?"

"Have him stay at the hospital tonight. His blood sugar is very high. Let it subside before he is discharged. Let's also give him some saline water to increase his energy."

"Sure," I said, nodding in approval. Jaya *dai* and I stayed in the same room with our father-in-law. It was seven in the evening.

"Let's do this. Why should we all stay here? Tell Kripa to bring me some food so I can stay here with *Buwa*. You all go home," Jaya *dai* said. "You can come in the morning and take care of him." It sounded like a good plan.

Kripa came to the hospital with a meal, leaving Krisha with Suman *didi*. My *sasuraba* ate a few morsels, and Kripa and I left after collecting the empty bowls, saying to Jaya *dai*, "Okay, we are going. Should anything else come up, please give us a call."

The next day, Dr. Prakash arrived at the hospital at noon and discharged my *sasuraba*. His sugar levels were normal by then. His face glowed a little bit—perhaps he wasn't in as much pain—and his saline levels were where they should be.

I managed to crack a few jokes and laugh, saying, "You are all set now, Father. Now you can rock and roll. When will we go out for whiskey and venison?"

He smiled.

After we got home, he talked with his grandchildren, Krisha and Araju, on the veranda, showing them things in the road—motorcycles and trash collectors. I looked at Kripa's face and found it surprisingly cheerful. I saw some hope in her eyes, despite the fact that his sickness was getting worse. I pictured the dwindling light of a lamp when the kerosene is about to run out. The brightness always intensified momentarily before fading away. The smile on my *sasuraba*'s face reminded me of that light. It made me reflect on the nature of change and how sickness can profoundly transform someone's life. Lost in these thoughts, my mind wandered for a while, contemplating the complexities of existence.

Life, I realized, is both beautiful and fragile.

Chapter Twenty-Three

Fate of Hamlet

December 30, 2019

The weight of my *sasuraba's* sickness and my wife's sorrow hung heavy in the air as I sat at her bedside. This invisible presence became a stark reminder of life's fragility and the inevitable dance with death. The room, once vibrant and alive, the room where I had dinner with the family, now exuded an air of somberness. Each shallow breath echoed the fleeting moments of existence. The gnawing ache in my heart intensified as I contemplated the unyielding grip of sickness, capable of altering lives in an instant. It was a cruel reminder that the strongest souls could be rendered helpless. In the midst of it all, a bittersweet realization washed over me – that our capacity to love and cherish one another was magnified in the face of mortality. The depth of human connection emerged as a beacon of hope, shining through the darkness. In that fragile moment, I vowed to treasure every fleeting second, for life's brevity and the specter of sickness held the power to transform our souls, reminding us of the preciousness of every heartbeat and the ephemeral nature of our existence.

Kripa asked once more, "Did you receive Jennifer's email?" It seemed as if Jennifer's email were the most important thing in her life right now, the center of her happiness. "What do you think, *Budho*? Will she allow you to teach from here in Nepal?"

"Let me check my email," I said, reaching out for my smart phone on the table. I turned the Wi-Fi on. I had already started doing yoga—*Anulom Vilom* and pandiculation. My father-in-law was still sleeping on his favorite red couch. "This is the best and most comforting place for me to sleep," I remembered him saying when I encouraged him to sleep in his bed. "I cannot go to the bed for your happiness."

There were many emails—mostly junk mail—but I saw there was one from Jennifer, the Dean of the Arts and Sciences department at my university. My heart beat raced with anxiety, wondering what she might have written. I prayed for her positive response before I started reading it.

Hello Tulasi,

I am so sorry all of this has happened. The only good I can see that has come from this may be that you were actually home in Nepal to comfort your wife and help with the logistics of the funeral and medical treatment of your father-in-law.

I have a couple of ideas up my sleeve to allow you to remain in Nepal for the Spring semester. I cannot make any promises and must speak with Dr. Peter about all of this first.

I apologize that I don't have an answer right away this minute, but I hope to have one tomorrow. I will write you as soon as I know anything.

Right now, please take care of and focus on your family, and I'll keep an eye on everything at work.

Pardon any typos as I'm on my phone,

Jennifer McClean, Ph.D.

Dean, School of Arts & Professional Studies

After reading through the email, I couldn't get much of a clear answer, nor could I allow myself to be hopeful. She had to ask Dr. Peter, the vice president of the college, for further information. I would have to wait for another email. I had only twelve days left before my flight back to the United States. With each passing day, Kripa was becoming more and more worried. She was feeling lonelier than ever. I put myself in her place and imagined how painful it would be for her if her partner weren't around at such as a tragic and mournful time. How vulnerable she might feel. I was also worried by the thought of living away from Kripa and Krisha when they needed my help. I felt I was the person most responsible for looking after them at this time. Krisha was still too young to know me as her father. These thoughts haunted me throughout the day. I longed to ease her pain, though I knew that healing was a deeply personal process that cannot be rushed. I held her hand and reminded her that she was not alone. I silently vowed to be her constant source of love and strength.

The day passed like any other day. Krisha spent time with her grandfather as usual. Whenever she found her grandfather nearby, she would forget everything else—except for her mother's milk. I had also heard that grandparents love their grandchildren the most, and since there wasn't a son in the home, they were more loving to their daughters and grandchildren. I remembered that in one of my research projects, an intriguing finding emerged: daughters played a more significant role in providing happiness and support to their parents compared to sons.

I didn't hear anything from Jennifer for the next two days. Kripa was the one who was most anxious about the email. I now had only ten days left before my return ticket to America. Every morning, as soon as she woke up, the very first question Kripa would ask me was, "Did Jennifer email you?"

"I don't give a damn right now whether I get an email or not. I would rather give up America and stay with you and Krisha. Baby, don't worry." I had become emotional with Kripa's frequent inquires.

My father-in-law heard me and responded feebly, his voice trembling:

"Everything has its course to run. Life must move on. You cannot leave the job that supports you and your family. Emotions don't last long—they come to comfort you, but decisions should be made with your rational mind and a clear understanding of practical necessities.

"Your wife needs you to earn enough to support her," my *sasuraba* said, turning to Krisha. "Think of your daughter and her future. We are aging and sick. I have no guarantee of my life. Now it is your time—and Krisha's time."

I listened to him quietly. His words were logical, practical, and painfully true. But as I considered the idea of leaving Kripa and Krisha behind in such a terrible situation, a wave of panic rose in me. The thought of returning to America without them felt unbearable.

"No, I won't go back to America. Whatever happens, happens," I said, repeating the words to Kripa as much to convince her as to steady myself.

"I'm not sure, *Budho*, how I can advise you," she said. "At times I think you shouldn't leave America, and other times I think we'll work hard in Nepal together and find joy in it."

For the moment, I decided I would rather live in Nepal and experience every bit of pain and joy with my family—caring for them, sharing life with them. That decision made Jennifer's email feel less urgent, less unsettling.

I thought about my daughter Krisha and her smile—playing with her tiny hands, pointing out stars in the evening sky while singing *Twinkle, Twinkle, Little Star* and *Tara Baji Lai Lai*. What could be more joyful than that? Being together as a family. Supporting Kripa and making her smile despite everything she had been through. I could take them to the countryside where I was born and raised—to show them the rhythm of rustic life, the simplicity of its people, and the little things that bring great joy. They could feel the thrill of harvesting crops with their own hands.

I wanted them with me, always—in my country, in my place—hearing my stories and living in the life I knew.

A Hamlet-like dilemma still hung over me.

Chapter Twenty-Four

News

January 2, 2020

My most important task every morning was to check my emails to see if Jennifer reached out to me. This morning, among the many emails was one from Jennifer. Again, my chest felt heavy with anxiety and fear. I took a deep breath, trying to relax myself. I invoked the name of God before I opened the email, realizing at that moment I could never be agnostic or atheist. I closed my eyes briefly and prayed, "Please, God, give me some good news." I tapped on the inbox to open it.

Hello Tulasi,

I apologize for taking so long to get back to you. In addition to your circumstances, there have been some other issues affecting the English schedule.

The good news is, the college will no longer be offering dual enrolled classes. This is the class you were to teach, so that has fixed itself.

I think you remaining in Nepal and teaching the 2 PBT classes, as well as creating the remaining classes, may be possible. Dr. Peter has asked for some more information, however:

Would you want and need to remain in Nepal for the whole Spring semester, or would you like to return to the college and teach the PBT classes during B Term? Had you planned to be in Nepal for Summer as well?

Can you please let me know your plans and preferences so that we can make an informed decision about Spring semester?

I hope you and your family are well under the circumstances.

Kind regards,

Dr. Jennifer McClean,

Dean, School of Arts and Professional Studies

After reading this email, my joy was endless. Now I could teach those classes from Nepal while being with Kripa, Krisha, my father-in-law, and my parents. I would still receive my monthly salary to support my own family. I wanted to tell this to Kripa, who was still sleeping. I silently kissed her on her forehead, and Kripa opened her eyes. Without a word to her, I showed her Jennifer's email.

She hugged and kissed me.

I think that was the first real affection I'd seen from her heart since she'd lost her mother. That pleased me. I told my father-in-law about the email after he woke up. He didn't say anything, but he shed a few tears of joy. In the afternoon, my parents called me from Kathmandu to ask about my father-in-law's condition, and I told them about my updates as well.

"Great!" they exclaimed.

I was overcome with a rush of elation and relief. A weight lifted from my shoulders as the knots in my stomach unraveled, replaced by a warm and comforting sensation. A wide grin spread across my face. It was a moment of pure joy, filling my heart with happiness and making me feel like I was floating on air. In that instant, all worries, doubts, and fears dissolved, leaving behind a sense of renewed self-confidence and belief in my abilities. The world seemed brighter, more vibrant, and filled with endless possibilities. Gratitude washed over me, and I felt a deep appreciation for those people who helped in the journey. It was a moment to cherish, a reminder to savor the positive in life and to embrace change. The satisfaction I experienced was indescribable, a mix of euphoria, relief, and gratitude that coursed through me.

Chapter Twenty-Five

Fear of Saturday

January 4, 2020

The sun rose over Pokhara like it always did—slow and golden—but something in the air felt unsettled. Kripa hadn't said anything yet, but I sensed her unease. It lingered in the way she held her teacup tighter than usual, the way her eyes followed Krisha toddling across the veranda with too much worry for a sunny morning.

"I should head back to Kathmandu," I said, watching steam rise from my own cup. "I need to prepare my spring courses. It's easier to work at my desk—with my books, my setup."

Krisha plopped down on her bottom and giggled. She reached for her mother's tea, stubborn in her toddler curiosity. Kripa didn't smile.

"When?" she asked, her voice almost casual.

"I can go today."

Her answer was immediate, almost sharp. "No. Not today."

Her father looked up from his special glass—the one he always used for milk tea—and nodded thoughtfully. "You know your work best. But if it can wait, perhaps don't go today."

I glanced at Kripa again. She was staring into her tea like it held an answer. Then she looked up at me—really looked—and said, "I don't want you leaving the house on a Saturday."

A silence fell. Krisha's babbling filled the space, but even that seemed far away.

I understood. Her mother had stepped out of the house on a Saturday. She never came back.

In that moment, fear didn't feel abstract. It wasn't a cultural construct or a conditioned belief passed down in stories of ghosts and unlucky days. It was love. It was grief. It was memory.

And it was real.

"I'll go Sunday, then," I said.

"Monday," Kripa whispered. "Please."

I nodded. "Monday."

She leaned against me, warm under the morning sun, and for a few seconds we just watched Krisha, who had found a leaf and was waving it in triumph. I felt the weight of departure press against the stillness of that morning. I wanted to stay in it forever.

But I also knew what Monday meant.

Chapter Twenty-Six

Attachment

January 6, 2020

I slipped my laptop and a few clothes into my backpack, along with the books I'd brought from home. Krisha and my father-in-law were still asleep beside me in the living room.

The thought of leaving—even for a few days—hit hard. I wanted to hug Krisha, to empty the bag and stay. But I had classes to prepare. A life to keep moving.

Robert Frost's words came to mind: *"Miles to go before I sleep."*

My job supported us. It wasn't just duty—it was survival.

Death could snatch us at any moment. I became emotional looking at Krisha and wondered when I would see her next, when I would hold her in my arms again. I already missed her so much, even if I was away for just an hour.

With the birth of Krisha, I had become more responsible. I felt a strong sense of fatherhood, a father's love. I realized that when someone becomes a father, he must become helpful, intelligent, compromising, sensitive, informed, and tolerant.

One tends to connect motherhood with the child. A mother keeps her child in her belly for nine months. It is not a simple task to be with the child constantly for nine months, carrying it in her belly, walking with it, interacting with it, experiencing bodily changes and going through the pain of labor to deliver the baby, and then to breastfeed them after that. This task is courageous and powerful and beautiful. One should also consider that being a father is not any less valuable, though he doesn't carry the child. Someone who has never had a child of their own can become a parent. Some people adopt children and care for them as their own, making them parents. When this responsibility enters the heart and head fully, anyone can be a successful parent. But when it comes to being the father of your own child, it means a lot—it means being able to listen to the child's heartbeat, to enjoy the child's joy, to be part of every aspect of the child's life and to enter the beautiful world they have created.

In Nepali society, being a woman is closely associated with getting married and becoming a mother. When a woman failed to meet those social standards that defined Nepali women, society looked down upon her. Due to the social structure we lived in, women tended to judge or define themselves through the social patriarchal lens.

Kripa had written an article entitled "Counseling Along with Prescription," published in the Annapurna Post, a national daily in Nepal. "To be a mother is a matter of good fortune for Nepali women. Those who become mothers for the very first time ... that day is truly special."

Yes, it is a fortunate thing to be a mother, whether there are social values that define motherhood as lucky or not, but what bothers me is the failure of understanding the meaning of being a father and the good fortune it brings. To have a child is a blessed thing in the lives of both the mother and the father.

I once read about attachment theory—the idea that a child's sense of safety and self-worth grows from early emotional bonds, especially with a primary caregiver. It began in the 1950s, rooted in studies of animal behavior and human development. Researchers say that when a caregiver is distant or unresponsive, a child may grow up feeling anxious, insecure, or unsure of their worth.

It struck me then—how much those early connections matter, and how often we overlook the father's role in that bond.

I remembered how Kripa had always admired her father and his personality. This was because a sort of attachment had been built between Kripa and her father. Although attachment theory underscored a mother's love toward her children, I realized that fathers didn't love their children any less than mothers. Anyone could be a father of a child, but after becoming a father, so many other aspects came into play. Being a good father required particular attention to one's own activities, demeanor, and manners.

As Krisha's father, I contemplated all those things while also thinking about my own father and fatherhood. I looked into Krisha's eyes, mulling over the pride of being her father.

Kripa brought black tea before I left for Kathmandu. I sipped it quickly before it turned cool since the weather was cold outside and there was no heat in the house. I didn't want to disturb my father-in-law and Krisha's sleep.

"If I manage my time well, I will be able to come back next week. Pokhara is not so far from Kathmandu anyway," I said, kissing Kripa before I left.

I took a local bus from Sisuwa and got off at Talchowk, one of the stations on the Prithiviraj highway. Seeing me standing by the station, a microbus driver shouted at top of his voice, "Kathmandu, Kathmandu, Kathmandu. Would you like to go to Kathmandu, *dai*?"

I got in the microbus. This route was more than familiar to me. I had driven it so many times that if it were clothes to wear, they would have been completely worn out. I had been back and forth on that route so frequently, especially after the death of my mother-in-law. I took out a book from my backpack, but no matter how much I tried, I couldn't get myself to read at all. To be candid, I never realized that a book could be read purely for entertainment. The only reason people read, I thought, was to gain information, knowledge about people and the world. Sometimes, people became so exhausted that they didn't want to learn anything at all. That is exactly how I felt, and I put the book back into my backpack. The scenes, mountains, hills, roads, buses, streams, and rivers: these all changed with time and the consciousness of the person who perceived them—Emmanuel Kant once said that nothing is the same and everything is in a constant flux. That feeling of constant flux made it difficult for me to concentrate on my books at that moment.

I reached Kalanki at two o'clock, and an hour later I was home. I rested for a few hours. In the evening, I had dinner and video called Kripa and Krisha, trying to tease Krisha, who wasn't interested.

I shared some updates with my parents and went to bed.

***

In the morning, I saw Jennifer's next email.

Hello Tulasi,

All the courses you teach in the Spring are online, so prepare accordingly. The classes begin next week, so don't forget to keep your students updated. Take care of your family, and if you have any questions, please let me know.

Kind regards,

Jennifer McClean, Ph.D.

I was even happier than before because now I had final confirmation that I could teach all classes online and stay with my family in Nepal. What a coincidence that the day I got her email was the day I was meant to return to America. Turkish Airlines must have called my name many times, I thought. I worked on my laptop, designing courses and other assignments. I had to meet with my students via Zoom.

***

A week had passed. I had prepared the materials for teaching, and the courses were already up on the online platform. I missed Kripa and Krisha a lot, and I didn't want to stay in Kathmandu any longer.

"I want to go back to Pokhara," I told my parents. I put everything—laptop, a few books and clothes—into the same backpack and rushed to Kalanki to catch a bus for Pokhara. My journey from Kalanki to Talchowk was smooth. I read a few books on the way, so my journey was quick and comfortable.

After I reached my father-in-law's house, I greeted them and asked them for updates. My father-in-law looked leaner, thinner, and worse than a week ago. His body was shrinking. Krisha acted like she knew me. She came up to me when she saw me. It made me so incredibly happy that no poet or a camera could ever have captured the feeling. I held Krisha and hugged her tightly.

"Daddy," she said. Tears of joy spilled down my cheeks.

Chapter Twenty-Seven

Dhido, Weed, and Manisha

January 13, 2020

Time doesn't stop for anyone. A month had passed since I returned to Nepal, and everything had shifted.

Most of my days were spent supporting my wife as she mourned her mother and cared for her ailing father. The weight of both losses pressed hard on her.

And I began to understand—really understand—what it meant to stand beside someone in their darkest hours, and how quietly that kind of love can wear you down.

Online classes had started through Zoom, and I had begun commuting back and forth from Kathmandu to Pokhara. On the weekdays I lived in Kathmandu, glued to my laptop while preparing my lessons, grading the assignments and teaching my online classes. On weekends I stayed in Pokhara with Kripa, Krisha, and my father-in-law.

"*Budho*, when you come to Pokhara next Friday, please bring some avocado," Kripa said, her voice tinged with sadness. "My father is willing to eat some. He won't eat anything else. He looks like he's shrinking—sinking a little more each day.

He's been saying his stomach pain is unbearable lately. I wonder if you could go see Dr. Ambuj Karna one more time and ask if there's anything we can do to ease his pain."

Kripa's eyes pleaded with me for help.

As soon as I hung up the phone, I went to see Dr. Karna at Bir Hospital. Since it was Monday, I could see him there.

"This is exactly what happens when you have this disease," Dr. Karna said. "People lose their appetite. If he still has pain, he needs to increase the dose of morphine. There is no other alternative. What are the total milligrams of the morphine he is taking now?"

"It is 30 milligrams, Dr. Saap."

"Let's increase it to 60 milligrams—one in the morning and one in the evening. He can take morphine syrup anytime he has pain. Along with that, he can take paracetamol every six hours. What we want is for the patient to be pain-free. This is palliative care."

"*My gosh, this morphine will be the cause of my father-in-law's death,*" I thought.

Later, I learned that the medication didn't cause death—it prolonged life. If the patient could eat and sleep, they would live longer and more comfortably, because the body wouldn't be under constant stress.

I looked at the doctor and said, "You had recommended giving him chemo, but the family was never ready for it."

"That's fine. But you must break the news," he said, as if he had now given up the idea of chemo. "Did you let your father-in-law know about his disease?"

"Not yet, Dr. Saap. The daughters don't want to disclose that. They think that it will cause their father more pain."

"What do you mean?" the doctor asked, his voice edged with fatigue. He looked worn down by the weight of patients and families like mine. "I'm giving you this advice because I've been in this profession for a long time."

"Yes, *Dr. Saap*, but how do I break it to him? It's terrifying news. What if he can't accept it—what if he faints?" I asked, placing the burden back on his shoulders, as if this were his responsibility to carry.

"You must tell the patient. Be blunt if you have to—rude. It doesn't matter. This is his disease. He has the right to know."

"I'll try my best, Dr. Saap," I said, and turned to leave, heading out to buy more morphine.

After I got home, I googled what patients of pancreatic cancer could eat to increase their appetite and lessen their pain.

Cancer patients, especially pancreatic cancer patients, have no appetite for food. If the food changed each time, there was a chance that the patient would eat a bit. I informed Kripa about that over the phone, so Kripa cooked different food with different flavors, such as Dhido, fish, and other items, changing the dishes every day, twice a day.

"Kripa tries to feed me good food and a variety of items, but she doesn't know how to cook them properly. Suman knows how to cook, but she repeats the same dishes, either rice, lentils, or curry," my father-in-law once complained when I spoke to him on a videocall.

"My father never used to complain before," Kripa and Suman *didi* said, full of understanding and worry. "These days, he has lost his patience and feels irritated. Perhaps it is the side effect of the disease and medicine."

My father-in-law liked *Dhido* a lot. "But they don't know how to cook it properly," he said. The next time I was in Pokhara, I cooked *Dhido* for him and served it. That time he liked it a lot. "The actual way of cooking *Dhido* is to put wheat flour into the boiling water and keep mashing it hard until it is fully cooked. You need to flex your muscles," my *sasuraba* said.

Suman *didi* also spent time looking for something that would lessen his pain or make him feel better.

"They say that if we give the cancer patient the soup of Gurjo, it will help. We should boil Gurjo and filter it through a strainer and let the patient drink its water," Suman *didi* said, and they started giving Gurjo water to him. She ordered Gurjo tea from the United States, asking her friends and relatives about it. The name on the packet was "Pure Graviola."

I spoke to some of my friends whose relatives had cancer and had recovered from it, but their cancer was of a different kind, and it was first or second stage. I called my friend Rajendra Pangeni, a cancer researcher at an institute in America, hoping for any thoughts on the matter. He discussed some theoretical aspects of the disease, but those wouldn't help with my father-in-law's cancer. Another friend, Hemraj Dhakal, whose mother was a cancer survivor, said, "My mother used ayurvedic medicine, making juice of Beetroot, white grass, Apple, carrots, Gurjo, and cow's urine. She is fine now."

We were willing to go to any length for a potential cure, even if it meant consuming something as unpleasant as cow's urine or other unconventional remedies. In fact, I believe that someone in his position would be willing to try anything if it held the promise of easing the pain.

After Hemraj mentioned ayurvedic medicine, it gave me a little bit of hope. I called Kripa immediately and asked her to give it a try. She managed to procure the medicine, but it didn't improve her father's health at all; in fact, he looked worse by the day. He stopped eating altogether, not a morsel of food.

I recalled hearing someone mention the potential benefits of using marijuana for cancer treatment or pain reduction, but I was unsure about the validity of such claims. It struck me that when faced with a dire situation, people may find themselves believing in illusions. To satisfy my curiosity, I turned to the internet and conducted a search: "Can marijuana help treat cancer?" The search yielded multiple results, and to my surprise, a significant number of them confirmed what I had previously heard about the potential benefits of marijuana for cancer patients.

After some reading, I learned that marijuana—specifically CBD oil—could help ease pain for cancer patients. I called a few friends to see if they could find some. But since weed is illegal in Nepal, no one wanted to talk about it on the phone. Eventually, I found a small bottle of CBD oil on Hamro Bazzar for ten dollars. I ordered it—along with a kilo of avocados, just as Kripa had suggested—and returned to Pokhara.

On the way, I thought of two books. *Healed*, by actress Manisha Koirala, and *Anatermanako Yatra* by Jagdish Ghimire. Both had faced cancer—one survived, the other didn't. But their reflections were strikingly similar. Cancer, they said, wasn't just suffering. It was awakening. It stripped life down to its essence, forced honesty, exposed regrets, and called for grace. In illness, they found clarity—how to live better, kindlier, more intentionally.

I arrived in Sisuwa on time. When Krisha saw me, she ran to me smiling—her first time without me calling her. My chest ached with joy. The video calls and weekend visits must be working. We were beginning to know each other. She was starting to see me as her father. And I was learning what that meant.

Every day she changed—her face, her body, her laughter. Watching her grow felt like witnessing a miracle unfold, one breath, one step, one smile at a time.

The days passed quickly. I moved between Kathmandu and Pokhara, taught my classes online, checked in with Kripa and Krisha, and did what I could for her father, even as his health slipped further away.

Chapter Twenty-Eight

Discussion of Patient's Rights

February 14, 2020

In Sisuwa, the cold loosened its grip by February. The heavy fog began to lift, and sunlight finally reached the veranda, where my *sasuraba* often sat and watched the hills. Mornings rang with the sound of temple bells, and the mountains stood still—silent observers, untouched by our daily worries. My father-in-law, meanwhile, stayed on his usual regimen of morphine, syrups, and paracetamol, trying to keep the pain at bay.

Even the increment of the additional morphine dosage didn't work, nor did the syrup to assuage my *sasuraba's* pain. At one point he cried out, "I am dying," so we rushed him to Gandaki Hospital in Pokhara and admitted him to the Emergency Department. The ED doctor, Dr. Dipak Shrestha, an oncologist, examined his condition.

Dr. Shrestha was in his early forties. Suman *didi* had talked to me a day before about the doctor and his desire to see the patient as well.

"He came across like a nice and very caring doctor to me," Suman *didi* had told me the other day. "He told me to 'bring the patient to me if he has a lot of pain. I will see what can be done.'"

When I finally met Dr. Shrestha, he didn't match the kindness Suman *didi* had described. I had come to know what a good doctor looked like—someone clear, present, human. This one spoke in circles, never smiled, and barely looked me in the eye. He never updated us, never asked how we were holding up. It felt like we were invisible unless we wore a white coat.

We admitted my *sasuraba* to ward eight—a room lined with eight beds, each holding someone worn down by cancer. Some patients were hooked up to chemo; others lay still beneath thin blankets, IV bottles swaying beside them. My father-in-law's neighbor, a frail man in his eighties with lung cancer, passed away just a month later.

Kripa's father stayed for three days. We gave him IV fluids, painkillers, and nutritional supplements. Dr. Shrestha suggested starting chemotherapy, but the daughters resisted. We still hadn't told him what he was facing.

"We have given chemo to people a lot weaker and older than him. Your father-in-law is just sixty-two. Let's try. Let's give him chemo," Dr. Shrestha repeated.

"The family is not ready yet, Dr. Saap," I said.

"As you wish," he said, not paying much attention to my words. I could understand why a doctor wouldn't want to hear that the patient or their family wasn't willing to follow the doctor's advice.

"Dr. Saap, we have not told him about his disease. We are worried about his confidence and hope for life, and he may not last much longer," I repeated the same statement I made to Dr. Karna, but the doctor pretended he hadn't heard what I said. My father-in-law's condition was deteriorating by the day, and I had no idea why I was talking gibberish about longevity. Perhaps I was trying to acknowledge the feelings of my wife and Suman *didi*.

Dr. Shrestha could have acknowledged me and said something in response. I found myself sympathizing with his difficult situation and the situation of other doctors like him.

Part of me thought, *Let's go ahead with chemo for my father-in-law.* But another part hesitated—he looked so fragile, I worried he might not survive it. I kept circling back to the idea of being honest with him, of telling him about the cancer so he could decide for himself whether he wanted treatment.

I remembered what Dr. Karna had said: "I think your father-in-law knows that he has cancer, but he is keeping silent because he doesn't want the family to be in pain." I decided that there was no point in keeping it a secret any longer. I thought it was the right moment to break the news. But the thought of going through with it hurt my brain. For the next three days, Jaya *dai* attended him during the night, and I looked after him during the day at the hospital. One night I googled the risks of chemo, and there were many. There were side effects, such as vomiting, loss of appetite, rashes and wounds on the mouth, diarrhea, constipation, bleeding, difficulty breathing...

I again thought of Dr. Karna, who had strongly recommended giving chemo to my father-in-law. I decided silently that I would let my father-in-law know, because each patient had the right to know their own condition. Dr. Karna had said this as well: "Your father-in-law has the right to know about his disease. Someone must break the news even if it seems rude or cruel."

I knew, deep down, that my father-in-law had a right to know. It was his body, his life. Still, I searched online, hoping to confirm what I already believed.

Most results focused on the U.S. The American Hospital Association's Patient's Bill of Rights—first adopted in 1973—guarantees a patient's right to clear information, to make their own medical decisions, to refuse treatment, to expect privacy, respect, and continuity of care.

In Nepal, the situation was different. Patient rights existed, but few people knew about them. Doctors often deferred to family, letting them decide what the patient should be told. They believed it was more compassionate that way.

But I knew we were wrong to keep it from him. I just didn't have the courage to tell him the truth.

I spent an entire night talking to Kripa and Suman *didi* about breaking the news, but I couldn't persuade them.

"We must let your father know about his disease. Look, I have already told you what Dr. Karna has said. It is also his right to know about his disease," I insisted.

"No," Kripa said. "What if my father becomes sadder and feels more pain?"

"What the heck are you talking about?" I said, frustrated. "What about the rights of the patient? How unfortunate would it be for someone to die without knowing the cause? After we explain this to him, he will decide whether to take chemo or not. Anyway, his life expectancy is coming to an end. You also must be mentally prepared for that."

I tried to be bold and brave. I had to be. I shook with fear while I spoke. I had also talked to Jaya *dai* about it previously, and he had agreed with me.

Silently, tears welled up in Kripa and Suman *didi's* eyes, streaming down their cheeks, enveloping the surroundings with an air of sorrow and tragedy.

I held strong. "No. This is not the time to cry but to make your heart strong and share this with your father," I said, mustering all my courage. "We've waited too long. A time has come to make a strong decision." I concluded the conversation right there.

Zenith, Araju, and Krisha had already fallen asleep. Jaya *dai* stayed at the hospital with my father-in-law.

In Suman *didi's* rented room, I lay on one of the beds, too restless to sleep. My body ached, but my mind kept circling—my mother-in-law's death, *Sasuraba's* condition, and the weight on his daughters.

It was February 14. Valentine's Day. And I hadn't even seen my wife.

I turned over again, helpless and exhausted, bracing myself for what tomorrow might bring.

Chapter Twenty-Nine

After Shedding Loads from the Heart

February 15, 2020

I didn't believe in destiny. But sometimes, life threw something at you that felt out of your hands—too sudden, too sharp to explain. In those moments, it's hard not to wonder if something larger was at play.

Still, we did have a choice. Not in what happened, but in how we carried it. That, I came to believe, made all the difference.

In the morning, I went to the hospital to take over for Jaya *dai* so he could have some rest or do chores after his night at the hospital. I promised myself I would break the news at any cost, though I felt dizzy at the thought of it.

"How should I tell him?" I mulled it over as I traveled to the hospital. The temperature outside was fifty-five degrees Fahrenheit, but the pressure within me was making my forehead sweat. My body felt warm. I was not thinking of anything other than how I could broach the topic and tell my father-in-law about his disease and the possibility of chemotherapy.

I walked into Ward 8. "Jaya *dai*, you can go home now. I am here now to stay with him," I said. Jaya *dai* was already up. How could he get any sleep in the hospital while all the patients around were shrieking and shouting? His eyes were red and he look tired.

Jaya *dai* left right away, saying, "Okay. If there is anything else, let me know." He also had to open the store, which was the only source of income for him to support his family and pay the rent and tuition fees for his children.

Now it was just my father-in-law and I at his bedside, along with the other cancer patients and their caretakers. My father-in-law woke up as soon as Jaya *dai* left, perhaps because of the noise of the patients, the custodial staff, and the general bustle in the hospital.

"How was your sleep, *Buwa*?" I asked.

"It was okay," he said. He was still in pain. I could tell from the way he pursed his mouth. "Why won't these people let me sleep? They keep making noises, and some of them even cry out, while others cough all night long."

The ward didn't feel like a place for healing. Though a few staff mopped with fennel water, the air still reeked—urine, sweat, and something darker, more primal. The stench clung to my skin, sharp and sickening. I thought, *even a healthy person might fall ill here.*

I couldn't help but remember hospitals in America—expensive, yes, but spotless. Carpeted hallways. One patient per room. Toilets that didn't make you flinch. There, the air carried the sterile sting of antiseptic. Here, it was thick with the raw scent of survival.

But without insurance, even that American comfort came at a cost most couldn't imagine.

I also remembered the time when my parents came to the United States in 2013. My mother became seriously ill and had to be hospitalized. The bill for just one night was $13,000. I was still paying it off, little by little.

Still, one thing stood out to me as remarkable: once a patient is admitted to the ER in the U.S., they don't have to leave if they can't pay. Treatment comes first. The bills arrive later, in the mail. It's a system that assumes care is urgent—and operates on trust that payment can be arranged later.

In Nepal, it's the opposite. Patients had to pay up front—no matter how serious the condition. Though medical costs were lower in Nepal compared to the U.S., most people couldn't afford the treatment with painfully low-income levels.

Unemployment remained high, and among the employed, only a small percentage earned a decent salary. Many families lived in poverty and struggled to pay hospital bills. The government didn't pay enough attention to the growing crisis.

"Did you feel stomach pain today, *Buwa*?" I asked.

"I didn't have any pain today, but they could not inject the IV in my hands. The saline didn't pass," he said. I looked at his hands. His skin was like a thin *pahade* paper, and I couldn't see the veins. They had disappeared completely. The saline water was not moving, his body unable to absorb anything.

How could his body bear the chemo? I asked myself silently. *Let it be. I will not bring up his cancer.* Then I thought again, *no, I must tell him. I should not violate his right to know about his disease.*

I started sweating from the internal conflict. I felt like I was fighting enemies on the battlefield with nobody to support me but myself. I finally decided to unfurl the knot. I wanted to know his opinion on the disease and the feelings he was going through. But once again I fell into a bout of indecisiveness, not knowing where to begin. I was confused.

"*Buwa*, would you like to have some breakfast?" I asked, delaying my own decision of whether to tell or not. "I can go to the cafeteria and bring something for you."

"Not now. I don't want to eat anything for now. If I feel like eating, I will tell you." He tried to adjust himself in his bed. He reached out for the bottle of Gurjo water on the small side table and drank it deeply, as if the water would save his life. He emptied the one little bottle of water within a minute, not even stopping to breathe. I saw his Adam's apple bob up down. It felt to me like he didn't want to die and was trying hard to come back to life.

Since all the patients in the ward had cancer, I guessed my father-in-law had some knowledge about it or had figured out about his own disease. Still, I wanted to be diplomatic and ask him in a roundabout way. "*Buwa*, do you know what kind of disease the people have in this ward?" I asked.

"Could be any kind," he said. Although he seemed to have no knowledge of their diseases, I knew my father-in-law was not the type of person who could sit quietly without investigating the situation around him. He must have already spoken to the patients on either side of him, or with their caretakers. Perhaps my father-in-law was pretending not to know in front of me and his family members.

"Has the doctor told you if this disease can be cured, *Buwa*?" I tried again with another question.

"Aren't they giving me these injections because they hope that I will be cured?" he questioned me more diplomatically, with a façade of complete innocence.

I felt helpless. What to say? How to say it? Unable to decide, confused and befuddled, I jumped up and went to the bathroom.

The stench hit me the moment I stepped inside—acrid, familiar, the same foulness that lingered in the ward. I couldn't manage to urinate properly, my body recoiling instinctively.

Only after returning to my *sasuraba's* bed, did I finally exhale the breath I'd held.

"Look, *Buwa*. The doctor has said that the stronger and braver you are, the more you can fight the disease," I said, inventing hope like it was medicine.

My *sasuraba* stayed silent and continued listening to me. "He said that the wound in your pancreas is way bigger than normal. If you are given chemo, there is a chance of it being cured."

I couldn't bring myself to mention the word "cancer," but at least I managed to gather the courage to say the word chemo. I was unable to look him in the eye while I spoke. When I finally looked up, he was leaning against the pillow with his eyes closed.

"Would you like to take chemo? The doctor strongly recommends it," I said again.

"No, I don't want it. Whenever the doctor says I am ready to go home, I would rather go home right away. I'm tired of the hospital," he said.

There was no surprise in his face—no reaction at all.

Did he already know? Did he think chemo meant certain death? Was he ready to join his wife?

Dr. Karna had suggested he might be aware, and now I wondered if he was right. A few moments later, Kripa arrived with Krisha. Whether my *sasuraba* knew his diagnosis before we spoke remained a mystery.

He was discharged on Sunday. We brought him home to Sisuwa. Jaya *dai* and Suman *didi* closed the store and came with us. We all were feeling sorrowful, so Jaya *dai* and I decided to ease our minds a bit.

"This has been a long period of hardship. Let's drink a bit, brother. What do you think?" Jaya *dai* proposed. Whether that proposal was meant to ease our pain or lift our spirits, I wasn't sure, but it sounded good to me.

That evening in Sisuwa, Jaya *dai* and I slipped out to a small restaurant packed with locals. Laughter echoed across the room. People drank, talked loudly, and let the night carry them. We ordered a few pegs of Khukuri rum and a plate of goat meat—trying, for a moment, to forget the heaviness we'd brought home.

As we sipped our drinks, Jaya *dai* spoke, the drink warming his words, "We must come to terms with our fate. I used to visit my in-laws every week, and the house was always brimming with laughter. But now, everything has changed. Nothing in this world is certain. I fear our *sasuraba's* time may be short. Our house is destined to mourn twice in a short span of time. What an unfortunate turn of events."

I took a swig of rum, and it burned going down. I grimaced—forgot to add water. That look alone answered Jaya *dai's* question.

We drank in silence. The warmth spread slowly, softening the edges of our grief.

Fate presented its path. But we didn't have to surrender to it.

We walked home lighter, not because anything had changed, but because we had decided not to let it break us.

Chapter Thirty

Morphine Invites Death

March 14, 2020

I was in Kathmandu in my house, reviewing my students' works. Krisha and Kripa were still in Pokhara looking after my father-in-law. "When Zenith's exam is over in a week or so, I will come and look after our father, and you can go to Kathmandu for a few days," Suman *didi* had said to Kripa. Therefore, I didn't make plans to go to Pokhara that weekend.

Everyone's thoughts were consumed by my *sasuraba's* cancer. It had reached its final stage—there was little hope left.

All we could do now was ease his pain, though even that grew harder by the day.

Still, I kept searching—hoping for an alternative treatment, a breakthrough, a miracle. I couldn't let go of the idea that something might still save him.

While I was sitting in front of my laptop, I decided to learn more about my father-in-law's pancreatic cancer. *Was it rare? Were there other notable people who had died from the same disease?* I googled using the command phrase "List of people diagnosed with pancreatic cancer." There was a Wikipedia page with this title. I perused and found that there were many renowned people and celebrities who were diagnosed with pancreatic cancer, and all of them had eventually lost their lives.

The list went on and on … I was stunned to learn that there were so many people diagnosed with pancreatic cancer. This was just a list of celebrities, and I could imagine how many people might be out there who might have been diagnosed with pancreatic cancer and had died unnoticed.

Still, I clung to stories of those who had outlived the odds—like Ruth Bader Ginsburg and Alex Trebek. They had battled pancreatic cancer and lived longer than expected. I wanted to know what treatments they'd tried, what made the difference. I searched for their medical histories, hoping to find something—anything—that might offer us a sliver of hope.

When I discovered that Trebek's stage-four cancer was treated and came back later, I had some hope for my father-in-law. Perhaps I should tell him to take the chemo, convince him to be strong and brave and confident. But his health had been completely jeopardized. He had started to look like a bag of bones. If he himself was not ready for it, there was no point in forcing him to go through chemo, either.

I tried to learn more—about survival rates, treatment outcomes, anything that might offer a way forward. But the more I read, the more I realized how much depended not just on medicine, but on the body's own strength—and the will to keep going.

My father-in-law had severe diabetes. Even when taking insulin, sometimes his blood sugar would go as high as 600. Once he had recovered from the ulcer operation, he continued drinking alcohol until it was too late, and he neglected his health.

I thought of taking my *sasuraba* to the most highly renowned cancer hospitals in Nepal, if that could bring some hope to his life. There were many well-known cancer hospitals in Nepal, such as Bhaktpur Cancer Hospital and Bharatpur Cancer Hospital. However, they were not particularly research-based. In the article "Fighting Cancer in Nepal—In Pictures," published in the Guardian on March 4, 2016, it was written that the "next step should include developing treatment centers throughout the country, establishing national research institutes and rolling out a nationwide registry."

***

Kripa video called me, showing me Krisha seated next to her. I lay on the bed and chatted with them. I felt relieved to have a small chat with Krisha, even though she could not yet talk.

"When are you planning to come to Kathmandu?" I asked. "I miss you guys so much."

"Suman *didi* will perhaps come here next week as soon as Zenith's exam is over," Kripa said. Her eyes held a longing to see me, eager for our time together, yet I could also sense her heartfelt desire to be with her father.

"That means around March 20 or 21?" I confirmed.

"Something like that."

"How is your father's health?" I asked, although I knew it was deteriorating.

"Even worse. Today he was trying to use the bathroom but fell on the floor and sprained his toes. He also got a scrape on his knee. I heard him fall and immediately went to lift him up. He sleeps a little but continues to have the same pain. He has stopped eating completely. When I see his body, I cannot control my tears. I've never seen my father looking so bony in my life."

Kripa swallowed hard, and tears rolled down her cheeks unchecked, stirring a wave of emotion within me.

There was nothing to be done—not from a distance.

Had I been beside her, perhaps I could have wiped those tears or rubbed her back. Instead, silence settled between us.

Sometimes tears had to fall—cleansing, purging—just as Aristotle once said of tragedy's power to evoke pity and fear.

Krisha, watching her mother cry, began to fuss.

"Don't worry, I'll call Dr. Karna and ask what might be done," I said, though I knew the truth—his time was near.

It's painful to watch someone die slowly. Still, I had to give Kripa something to hold on to. Even if I'd lost hope myself, I needed to offer her just enough to keep going.

Sometimes, that's all hope is—something we offer for someone else, even when we no longer carry it for ourselves.

I phoned Dr. Karna.

"If he is still feeling pain, we need to increase his dose," Dr. Karna said. "Yes, of course, someone with pancreatic cancer won't have an appetite for food. And the morphine also makes the patient's appetite go away. Now increase the dose from 60 to 90 mg and continue to take paracetamol every six hours, three tablets each time." He refrained from discussing any alternatives and instead opted to continuously increase the doses, leaving it as the only remaining solution.

I silently whispered in exhaustion and thought that it was not the cancer but the morphine that was killing my father-in-law so quickly. *Morphine*, I thought, *was a slow poison, which might not be right for cancer patients.*

"If that doesn't help him, we should again increase the dose," Dr. Karna said. That scared me to death, and I chuckled to myself like a mad man.

Dr. Karna's suggestion to increase the dose if the current one didn't provide relief unsettled me and I felt goosebumps prickling my skin.

Dr. Karna even mentioned that some patients took as much as 1,000 mg of morphine, which made the 90 mg dose seem insignificant by comparison.

"Thank you, Dr. Saap," I said, hanging up the phone. My brain was unable to fathom what he had said.

My search on the internet had shown much the same results. "Such a fearful and lethal disease cancer is," I murmured to myself.

The call to Kripa came immediately, urging her to increase the morphine dose.

She resisted, not yet understanding that enduring such pain could be more harrowing than death itself.

Her face on the video call had lost all its color, draining the breath from my chest.

A silent prayer rose—*may she find her way back to herself soon*, though more suffering still waited ahead.

"Why the hell are you trying to be a doctor? Just do what the doctor has said—or let your father suffer the pain," the words came sharp, love masked beneath the frustration.

"There is no other alternative."

Comfort should have come instead, but anger took its place.

Fatigue pressed down heavily, feeding a helplessness that bled into every word.

Kripa started weeping, her eyes brimming with tears.

"*Budho*, can't we take my father to India—or anywhere else—where we could treat him and get him back to his normal self? I could at least feel content having my father alive for another few years, so these growing kids could have quality time with their grandfather."

She looked from Krisha to me and back again.

"We've become orphaned too early. Even if my mother is gone, my father could have lived a little longer—so I'd have a piece of her in him. I'm even ready to sell this house to afford his treatment. I don't care about money or property. I just want my father to live a few more years."

Her words unraveled me—tears welled, and my heart shattered under the weight of her plea.

No answer came. Her request stuck like a stone in the throat, too heavy to move.

With what little strength remained, a quiet performance began—pretending everything was fine, though nothing was.

"This is not a matter of money, *Budhi*. If we could treat him, we could take him and spend any amount of money. This is the type of disease that cannot be cured at this stage," I said.

"So, money means nothing now? What kind of disease is this?" Kripa retorted, although she knew very well what kind of disease it was.

Encouragement came gently—urging her to continue with the remedies they'd been using: Gurjo water, ayurvedic medicine, CBD oil—and, above all, to nourish her father with flavorful meals and steady moral support.

Her tears flowed freely, reflecting a pain too deep to fully grasp.

"And how is Krisha doing?" The question came in an attempt to steady the heart and shift the weight of the moment.

"She is taking a nap,"

"And father?"

"He is also sleeping. He only sleeps, as if he will never open his eyes again," she said, squeezing her eyes shut and pursing her lips to hold her tears back.

"Please take care of Krisha and look after yourself, too. Now Krisha is both your father and mother," I said, hanging up quickly before she could see the tears in my own eyes.

Eyes drifted to the ceiling while lying on the bed.

The room hadn't been touched since Kripa's mother passed.

In the corner, a cobweb hung undisturbed, its fragile threads still catching the light. The fly once trapped there was gone—no trace left, not even a wing.

That empty web became something more than dust and silk—it was the shape of life itself: how we struggle, how we hold on, how we vanish.

What had once been a place of capture now held only absence. And in that absence, the quiet outline of death.

A call from my mother broke the stillness, summoning me upstairs to eat. She and my father asked gentle questions about the state of my father-in-law.

"I am dying to see Krisha, at least on video," she said, placing food on the table with a kind of longing only a grandmother can carry.

"Perhaps they will come to Kathmandu next week and you can play with her," I said, shoveling the food into my hand and forcing myself to eat.

After finishing the meal, I spent some time on the laptop grading the students' papers and assignments. I had to present a paper in the seminar next week, so I prepared a bit for that task.

After grading a few papers and outlining my seminar notes, I stepped outside for some air. The mountains stood quiet and steady in the distance, their silence somehow reassuring. I let my eyes rest on their outline, drawing strength from their presence—unchanging, even as everything else felt fragile.

We couldn't stop death or outrun it. But we could hold tight to the moments that mattered. The laughter around a dinner table. A hand held during a hard night. Time with the people we loved—that's the part of life that stays with us.

In the shadow of loss, those memories shone even brighter. They reminded me what it meant to truly live. As I sat with those thoughts, one truth settled in my heart: love was the only thing we could carry forward.

I missed Kripa and Krisha deeply. I ached for the next time we'd be together.

Chapter Thirty-One

Fear of COVID-19 and Hope for a Miracle

March 14, 2020

The pandemic had spread across the world like wildfire in a dry jungle, with large numbers of fatalities in Italy, America, and Spain. The government of Nepal also recognized the seriousness of the situation and imposed a nation-wide lockdown. The government lockdown was meant to last for one week, immediately after the virus began to spread. People were allowed to walk and travel within their own district, but they could only travel by plane in the case of an absolute emergency.

As the virus that began in Wuhan spread across the world, fear seeped into daily life. By late January, Nepal was no exception. The numbers rose quickly, and so did the tension. Cities locked down. Masks became a way of life. The streets emptied, but the worry was everywhere.

Kripa and Krisha were on their way to Kathmandu from Pokhara.

The thought of seeing them again stirred deep happiness. But beneath that joy lived the awareness that Kripa would still be mourning—missing her father, carrying the fresh loss of her mother.

A meeting with students was scheduled for four Tuesday morning in Nepal—the equivalent of six fifteen in the evening on Monday in the United States. Preparation for the session was already complete: PowerPoints finalized, materials reviewed, lectures delivered.

The next meeting wouldn't come until the following month. Students who had questions could reach out by email in the meantime. Weekly updates, announcements, and assignment grading would continue online, maintaining the rhythm of remote teaching even as life in Nepal pulled the heart elsewhere.

In the morning, Kripa called me and said, "Should I come to Kathmandu or not? There is a rumor of a lockdown across Nepal. They are saying no one will be allowed to travel across the district. If I come to Kathmandu and cannot come back to Pokhara, what will I do? Right now, the planes are allowed to fly, but what if they stop the planes from flying?"

Kripa was right. But I was not listening.

"What are you talking about, Kripa? You've been in Pokhara for a long time now. If Suman *didi* is coming to take care of her father, why don't you take a break and come home? I am missing you guys so much. How long can I continue to go back and forth every week, spending all this time and money? More than anything else, I need to save some time and at least have a little break with my family. Here, I am teaching the students online. In Sisuwa, I might not have internet all the time. If Zenith's exam is over, and Suman *didi* is saying she will look after your father, then come," I said. "If you still think that Suman *didi* cannot or doesn't have time, that's fine, you do not have to come. I will come instead."

"Again, they are saying that the whole country is under lockdown and we will not be allowed to fly. If that happens and something happens to my father during the lockdown, I wonder whether I would even be able to get back to see him or not," she repeated.

"If that happens, we can find an emergency vehicle or something like that. Please do not stress out right now?" I tried to address her problem, my face looking stern. In truth, I desperately wanted to see them as soon as possible. "If possible, please book the plane ticket and come to Kathmandu as soon as you can."

"I am in a dilemma. Krisha is also coughing as if she has Covid," Kripa said. As soon as I heard that, my heart raced faster. One of the primary symptoms of COVID-19 was a bad cough. The person would have a breathing difficulty and could die. I was scared thinking that my one-year-old daughter might have COVID-19. I wanted Krisha to be with me as soon as possible.

"Whatever you want to do, Kripa, it is up to you," I replied, my mind racing with thoughts. My response sounded very rude. Kripa felt an urgency to come to Kathmandu, thinking that I was very angry. Since the country was under lockdown, Kripa had already asked her journalist friend to give her a ride to the Pokhara airport and was ready to come to Kathmandu. She video called me from the airport. It was quiet. The airport was always filled with passengers, but this time it was only Krisha and Kripa.

"Aren't there other passengers?" I asked.

"No. Some are coming in one by one, but it is almost empty," Kripa said.

Both wore facemasks. Poor Krisha, too young to understand, kept tugging at hers, trying to remove it.

A rush of thoughts flooded in.

What if she caught the coronavirus and became sick?
Should they have stayed in Pokhara?
They should never have been asked to come to Kathmandu at all.

"Please make sure to maintain social distancing. Look after Krisha," the reminder came gently.

The plane was scheduled to depart for Kathmandu in half an hour.

Preparations began for me to leave for the airport.

On the way, two policemen stopped the scooter and asked about the journey. A brief explanation was enough to receive a nod of approval. The scooter was parked in the airport lot, and the wait began.

About thirty minutes later, the plane landed.

Kripa emerged from the terminal with Krisha in her arms, a mask covering her face. Nearly a month had passed since we'd last seen one another in person.

Sanitizer was pulled from a pocket and rubbed into both hands.

Krisha was gathered into a loving embrace, and gentle hands reached out to rub the backs of both mother and child.

Blessing and joy surged—wordless and full.

The urge to kiss Krisha's cheeks, forehead, eyes—held back.

Fear of COVID-19 created a barrier between love and touch, muting the expression of affection that longed to overflow.

Their small bags were placed on the front of the scooter.

Kripa climbed on behind; Krisha nestled safely between us.

Together, we made our way home to Tikathali.

Kripa informed Suman *didi* that she had arrived. It was noon. My parents washed their hands with soap and hugged Krisha out of joy from seeing her. Krisha had started saying, mummy, daddy, papa ...

Kripa ate the lunch my mother had made and lay down on the bed for some rest. I rested on the bed with her. Krisha breastfed while napping. We all remained there for a while.

The sense of relief that washed over me as I was reunited with my beloved wife and daughter, all of us together in one bed, was overwhelming. I embraced them tightly, savoring the warmth of their presence. Closing my eyes, I felt an indescribable joy filling my heart. In that precious moment, I realized how much their love meant to me, and how blessed I was to have them by my side. It was a feeling of contentment and gratitude, knowing that I had returned to the embrace of my cherished family, where happiness and love were shared unconditionally.

"And how is your father now?" I asked, the same question that had become part of our daily rhythm.

"After taking the CBD oil, he seems to feel better, but sometimes he cannot tolerate that either. He eats a morsel or two sometimes. I have a feeling that the CBD oil is helping his appetite. He spends some time watching the neighbors' playing cards. I would give him a few slices of kiwi and apple. He is always drinking Gurjo water."

Hearing this brought a wave of relief—hope flickered again for his life expectancy.

Pride swelled quietly for Kripa, whose love for her parents ran deeper than anything else.

"It feels good listening to you," the reply came warmly. "And didn't Krisha cry while leaving her grandfather?"

"Yes, she was saying 'baa, baa,' but my father couldn't even respond to her calling him. He became teary at the thought of her leaving. He looked away from her as he said 'Goodbye,'" Kripa said. "He was saying 'Your daughter is so intelligent. My presence will be enough for her to understand.'"

"You never know. Your father might make a full recovery and return to normal. Listening to you, I have some hope now," I said, although I knew this could never be true.

As we lay on the bed talking, half falling asleep, Krisha woke us up. It was five in the evening. Kripa made dinner. I wanted to tell her to rest and let my mother cook, but I started to worry that my mother would complain, saying, "He let his wife rest and made me cook."

My mother was not the type of person who would ever say such a thing, but you never know about the mother-in-law and daughter-in-law relationship in Nepali society. My mother was ill and took medication every day. *It's a tricky thing to be the only son of Nepali parents*, I thought.

Kripa served all of us our evening meal, and after we finished eating, we came downstairs to our own bedroom.

Some time passed as I scrolled through my phone.

Kripa called her sister Suman and spoke to her father.

Krisha's voice echoed softly through the video call: "Baa ... baa ..."

On the screen, Kripa's father's eyes filled with tears. He became so emotional he couldn't speak, turning his face away from the camera.

His frail body shocked me—a stark contrast to the image I still carried from before, his strength now worn thin by illness.

The toll was written clearly in the lines of his face and the bones beneath his skin.

It was hard to see him like that.

Even though Kripa said he had begun eating a little more when offered food with different flavors, I couldn't imagine how much longer he could endure.

And yet—across that fragile screen—his silence told us he was still holding on.

Chapter Thirty-Two

Fear, Horror, and a Day of Disturbance

April 4, 2020

We had been in lockdown for weeks. The silence outside was eerie—no school bells, no market noise, just the occasional bark of a stray dog. Inside our home, we kept our distance. We wore masks, washed our hands, and spoke in lowered voices, as if the virus could hear.

Everywhere, the news screamed of rising death tolls. People were dying without oxygen, without beds. It didn't feel like modern life—it felt like something out of a Greek tragedy.

Even in our home, fear lived in the corners. We sanitized door handles and rationed food. And beyond our walls, people were walking for days to return to their villages. Some didn't make it. Some gave up.

The sadness was everywhere—on the screen, in the streets, and inside our hearts.

Nepal's government extended the lockdown for another fifteen days, this time more strictly than before. No one was allowed to leave the house during curfew, with only a few hours in the evening to shop for groceries and other essentials.

The fear crept in quietly, then took hold. I started imagining worst-case scenarios—*what if I lost Kripa? What if Krisha got sick and I couldn't help her?* The thought of it made my chest tighten.

They were my whole world. Without them, nothing else mattered.

Even as my heart broke over *Sasuraba's* declining health, the rising death toll from COVID-19 left me restless, afraid, and hollow. The future felt fragile. Every moment felt like it could be the last.

I just wanted to keep them safe. But I didn't know how.

One morning during the strict lockdown while we were having breakfast, Suman *didi* called around nine in the morning and spoke to Kripa.

"And how is father?"

"What can I say, Kripa? He finds it more difficult to live every day," Suman *didi* said.

"What happened?" Kripa asked. "He was fine—a bit better when I left him. He had started eating again, even if it was only a little bit."

"I agree. He was eating well until the day after you left, but now he's completely stopped eating anything. I didn't tell you this earlier because I didn't want to bother you. His hands shake while injecting the insulin and he cannot do it properly. He fell on the floor on the way to the bathroom this morning. He finds it difficult to swallow his morphine medicine," Suman *didi* said.

As soon as Kripa heard this, the tears spilled from her eyes. I massaged her back with love and care. She cried more, perhaps releasing her pain with my sympathy.

"Don't fret! We cannot do anything during the lockdown. Let's wait. If something serious happens, we will take him to the hospital," Suman *didi* said before ending the call.

Kripa turned on me, her voice trembling with rage.

"I told you I didn't want to come to Kathmandu during the lockdown. Now my father will die, and I won't be able to see him. If I was there with him, perhaps he would live a bit longer. He was eating when I was there. I had to come to Kathmandu because of you!"

Frustration rose before any compassion could surface.

"Why are you angry with me? I told you to do as you liked," the words escaped, sharp and defensive.

Beneath it all, a hollow ache deepened—the sense that no one saw how much had been carried, how much had been done for this family, silently and without rest.

"You were obviously angry when you said that. What else could I do?" Kripa said.

"That is just the way I speak."

Hearing the rising tension in our voices, Krisha began to cry.

She was gathered into my arms and held close against my chest, rocked gently in an attempt to soothe her.

"Why are you so stressed out?" The words came out more harshly than intended. "I've already told you to prepare for your father's death. It could happen at any moment—his illness can't be cured. Please, try to have patience. If we need to go to Pokhara, I'll find a way. I'll hire an ambulance if I have to. But breaking down now won't help anyone."

The tone carried more edge than comfort.

It was the voice of someone scared, someone human—exhausted from doing a million things, stretched thin, and unsure how to hold it all together.

After I spoke, Kripa calmed down and stopped crying. She took Krisha upstairs in the kitchen to feed her some *lito*.

The whole day, I phoned Suman *didi* and inquired about her father's status. Kripa spent the day depressed, worried, stressed, lying on the bed and looking blankly at the ceiling.

"If there was no lockdown, I would have already gone back to Pokhara, *Budho*. My heart is racing," Kripa said, holding my hands.

A hand moved slowly along her back, a small gesture of comfort, while Krisha received playful attention to lift the heaviness in the room.

After hearing what Kripa was going through, my parents joined in—offering quiet words and presence to ease her pain.

"Please be patient. We can find an ambulance tomorrow and go to Pokhara," I said.

In the evening, I sat down to watch the news on TV, and it became evident that the contagion had seeped into every corner of the world, leaving a trail of devastation in its wake. The death toll continued to rise, and the fear surrounding the virus was palpable. Every piece of information echoed fear. As the reports unfolded before me, a chilling terror crept down my spine. It wasn't just me; anyone who came across these updates or read about the pandemic in the newspapers couldn't help but feel a deep sense of anxiety and apprehension about the uncertain times we were living in. The rampant infection had cast a dark shadow over humanity, leaving us all feeling vulnerable and seeking reassurance amidst the uncertainty.

Chapter Thirty-Three

Pass, Breath, and Hope in Lockdown

April 5, 2020

Kripa jolted awake, clutching me hard, her breath ragged and uneven.

"I—" She swallowed. "I'm ... so scared, Budho." A gasp. "Last night ... the dream—" Her voice broke, and a shuddering sob escaped. She pressed her face into my shoulder.

"I can't lose him." The words came in pieces, splintering. "I feel like I'm breaking. Like I might ... collapse."

Another breath, sharp and shaky. "Having you here ... is a lifeline. I cannot fathom ... how I'd cope without you. Your presence anchors me." She gripped me tighter, her voice barely more than a whisper. "Without it... I'd feel shattered into pieces. Thank you... for being my rock."

Her eyes lifted to mine, brimming. "But today... today feels worse. Different. I worry my father might be in a bad state."

Her hand trembled as she reached for the phone. She pressed the call through, the screen lighting at eight in the morning.

"How... how is Father?" she asked, the question breaking apart on her lips.

Suman's response was filled with fear. She expressed her anxiety about their father's deteriorating condition, her husband's presence being the only thing keeping her from breaking down. She felt guilty for Kripa's decision to go to Kathmandu, wondering why her husband (that is me) had encouraged it in the first place.

Suman *didi's* voice trembled as she described their father's deteriorating state. He looked worse than the day before, and the sleepless night had taken its toll. She spoke of his confusion, how he muttered incoherently, struggling to stay upright, often forgetting where he was trying to go. When asked, he would say he wanted to go to bed but would end up in the toilet instead. The weight of the moment settled over her; she feared he might not see another sunrise. With urgency, she pleaded for Kripa to return to Pokhara immediately, recalling the last time when Kripa had only seen their mother after she had passed. Suman couldn't bear the thought of Kripa missing their father this time.

As Suman spoke, tears streamed down Kripa's cheeks. Krisha, sensing the heaviness in the air, began to cry, calling out for her *mamu*.

A surge of anger rose at Suman *didi's* words—blame aimed in my direction—but it was quickly recognized for what it was: the voice of grief.

Their father's condition had opened a floodgate of unfettered emotion. Stepping into the living room, I quietly dialed Jaya *dai's* number.

"How is his condition, *dai*?" the question came, barely above a whisper.

"I don't think he will last too long, Tulasi," he replied. "I don't know what to tell you because there is the lockdown, and I don't think it will be easy for you to come."

The message was clear. The call ended quickly.

Back in the room, Kripa's tears flowed freely as she continued speaking with her sister—grief spilling over, too heavy to contain.

Beside her, Krisha began crying too, a child absorbing her mother's sorrow as if by instinct.

"You found our mother after she was already dead. I wanted to make sure that you would be here before our father died," Suman *didi* repeated, her words echoing in the background.

Kripa's entire demeanor had shifted.

She looked fragile, trembling—hands and legs unsteady, her body visibly bracing for the pain of her father's passing.

"If you keep talking like this, I won't be able to do anything to help," I snapped, my voice sharper than I intended. "You knew about your father's situation. Yes, it's a terrible event, but you know the disease he has, and you knew this day was coming. Please be calm, and let's do what we can. Let's find out how to get to *Pokhara*. I'll call for an ambulance. You reach out to your friend to see if there's a way we can get there. If we can prove it's urgent, there might be a chance to travel during the lockdown," I said, adrenaline tightening my chest.

After that, Kripa tried to remain quiet, swallowing her sobs as she began calling her friends.

I dialed the digits 1-0-0.

"If it is only within the Kathmandu valley, we will go. Otherwise, we cannot come to your aid," they said.

I realized the totality of the lockdown when I heard that even the emergency vehicles wouldn't travel to us. It made me very angry. The Nepalese government should at least allow the ambulances to travel outside the valley if it was an emergency. A weak government's helpless citizens, I thought to myself, venting my anger. *Such bullshit.*

Kripa also called her journalist friends in Kathmandu and Pokhara. They all said, "We will try, but it is difficult." Even if we found the car, we would have to pass the police stops on the way. Kathmandu's district administration office would give us a permit, depending on the urgency of our case, otherwise we wouldn't be able to proceed. She called the assistant chief district officer, Tulasi Poudyal, who had recently moved to Kathmandu district administrative office. She had known him for a long time and asked for authorization.

A weak attempt at levity slipped out: "Looks like people named Tulasi bring good things into your life, huh?"

But this was no time for teasing, and Kripa didn't smile.

Tears streaming, she spoke into the phone, her voice shaking.

"Sir, my father's condition is very critical. He is dying. I must go to Pokhara, and I don't have a permit. I am also looking for a taxi. Can you please find me a permit?"

Unfortunately, he was away from the office that day.

"Kripa *jee*, I have just one here with me, but this is for one of my friends who had requested it the other day. I am in a difficult situation now."

She sobbed into the phone, repeating her request. Her misery made his heart melt. "It's okay, Kripa *jee*. You've cried a lot. I will write your name here. Please come and take it," he said on the loudspeaker.

She thanked him through her tears.

"Did you find a car, though?"

"Not yet. Still looking for one."

"We have a tenant in my house who drives a taxi. I will talk to him. I will call you back right away."

In a few minutes, the officer called Kripa on her phone and said, "He will charge you $170 dollars to go to Pokhara. Is that okay?"

In this situation we would have paid $1,000, let alone $170, so she said right away, "That's fine."

Getting Kripa to Pokhara became the only thing that mattered.

In that moment, the harsh truth settled in: money mattered.

Without it, even the deepest love or strongest will couldn't cross the distance. Money isn't everything—but in times like this, it is undeniably something.

The house of the district officer was not far from our own house in Tikathali, about fifteen minutes away on foot. Krisha was already awake, so we packed our clothes and Krisha's too, putting together two small bags and a suitcase, and we put everything in them, including the laptop I couldn't live without. We put our masks on, carried sanitizer, asked my parents for their blessing to leave, and walked to Tulasi Sir's place to get the pass and taxi to go to Pokhara. Although we were scared of COVID-19, in that moment we had no other care besides our goal of reaching my *sasuraba*.

"Can't you leave Krisha with us?" my mother asked. "It will be difficult for you, and especially for her, during the lockdown."

"We would, but she is just one year old and will miss me. She also needs to be breastfed. She would be looking for me in the night," Kripa said.

Kripa was desperate to get to Pokhara.

With all our bags, we arrived at Tulasi Sir's place. He stood waiting, permit in hand, a taxi already prepared for our departure.

A flicker of fear passed through me—what if Krisha caught COVID-19? She couldn't wear a mask properly and wouldn't keep it on.

Her innocent face held my gaze for a moment, so full of trust and unknowing love.

There was no doubt—she was loved more than life itself.

We took the ticket, thanked Tulasi Sir, and climbed into the taxi.

Despite the driver's assurance that it had been cleaned, every surface was sanitized once more.

Masks were tightened, doubled up.

And with hearts pounding, we rushed toward Pokhara.

At Nagdhunga, after we passed Kalanki, the police stopped us. We showed him the decree that stated Kripa's father was dead. We were told that if we mentioned he was dead, there might be a chance for the police to let us go. Otherwise, they wouldn't, regardless of the emergency. We lied to them that he was already dead, though we knew full well he was going to die anyway.

After we passed Nagdhunga, the winding roads in Thankot began. Krisha immediately started vomiting all over Kripa's body and looked very weak. Her little feet and body were icy to the touch. My heart pounded against my chest like a relentless drum, and my breaths grew shallow and erratic. A cold sweat broke out on my forehead, and my hands trembled uncontrollably. It was as if a thousand needles were piercing my skin. Every nerve in my body on edge. A primal fear clawed its way up from the depths of my being, threatening to engulf me entirely. The sensation was so overwhelming that words failed me. My heart felt as if it would pound right through my chest. So many thoughts came to my mind. *Did she have COVID-19? My mother suggested leaving her at home, but we didn't listen. What would happen to my daughter?*

Kripa was more worried about her father, but seeing her daughter in such a state, she began to look scared, too. My hands shook as I told the driver to stop the taxi.

Krisha had vomited all over her clothes, by the door of the taxi, and onto the seat. The weather was getting warmer, but not hot enough to explain the sweat on her forehead. I took a bottle of water from my backpack and began cleaning the mess—from the door, the seat, and Kripa's clothes.

A gentle breeze from the Thankot hills cooled us slightly. After five minutes, Krisha's face looked better, and her skin felt normal again—her hands and feet had warmed. She even started to speak. The beat of my heart slowed to its usual rhythm.

Tears rose to my eyes. She was okay. It wasn't COVID-19, just motion sickness from the endless curves along the hills.

Still, before we reached Pokhara, Krisha vomited three more times. My poor little girl—she had to suffer through all of this.

I looked at her and thought, *you also have to face this fate—to lose your grandparents, to suffer with us, and never even get to celebrate your first birthday.*

On the way, we became true witnesses to the lockdown. We had to stop at fifteen different checkpoints on the way and were asked to show the pass—they measured our body temperature at every stop and asked many questions. We had to lie to them that my *sasuraba* was dead. We had left Kathmandu around nine in the morning, and it was two in the afternoon by the time we got to Sisuwa.

A throng of people had gathered—neighbors, relatives, and familiar faces like Laxman *dai*, Jaya *dai*, and Suman *didi*—all there to see my father-in-law.

He lay on the floor in critical condition, barely recognizable.

Crawling in slow, circular motions like a tortoise, he seemed trapped in a body that no longer listened to him.

The sounds he made weren't words, only fragments of something lost.

For a fleeting moment, an image from literature came to mind—Kafka's *Metamorphosis*. In the story, the man wakes up transformed, helpless, lying upside down, unable to move.

My father-in-law's condition echoed that horror—not in fiction, but in front of my eyes.

Just a week ago, he had seemed okay.

Now, in a matter of days, the disease had hollowed him out, and the morphine had changed him further—dulled his body, dulled his presence.

The transformation was almost beyond belief.

Krisha, seeing her grandfather, ran forward, calling "Baa ... Baa ..."—eager to play, to be near him.

But he could no longer respond.

Fear rose in me—so many people, so little protection.

What if one of us caught COVID-19?

I didn't want Krisha in the crowd, didn't want her that close.

But how could I stop her?

She only saw her grandfather.

Not the tragedy.

Not the dying.

There was no easy way to bear it.

No words for what it felt like to witness a life unravel before us.

It was terrible—unthinkable—and yet somehow, it was real.

"Let's not gather too closely at this time of COVID-19," I said to the people, the villagers thronging there. Kripa cried as she watched her father.

Kripa was held, comforted, and chided. "Have you started again?" I asked, trying to steady her. "Nothing is under your control now. Your tears won't cure your father. Let me talk to the doctor and see what they say."

A call was placed to Dr. Kharal, updating him on the rapid decline in my father-in-law's condition.

The concern was made clear—things had grown far more serious.

Dr. Kharal's response was direct. He suggested that the cancer might have spread to my father-in-law's brain and, despite not being a cancer specialist, he recognized the gravity of the situation.

Desperate for hope, I asked if we could take him to the hospital. Deep down, I knew it would likely be futile. Dr. Kharal advised that we could go if we wished, but it was too late for chemotherapy—our visit would be more for our own comfort than for any medical benefit. After our conversation, I hung up, the weight of his words echoing in my mind.

I shared the harsh truth with them.

"There is no use taking him now, *Jwaisaap*," Laxman *dai* added. "This lockdown and the spread of COVID-19 might make us all sick, so it's better to be cautious."

Jaya *dai* seconded the idea of staying put.

Suman *didi* gave me the phone number of Dr. Prakash at Lekhnath Community Hospital. I requested that he come to the house and see the condition of my father-in-law. He showed up very quickly and, upon seeing the patient, said "You don't need to bring him to the hospital. No point at all. Even if you bring him there, they will put him in ICU and take him out only after he stops breathing. Here at least you all are with him. You can see him and be with him to the end."

Kripa suggested performing *Baitarani*, and everyone readily agreed. In our culture, this ritual holds deep spiritual and symbolic meaning. *Baitarani*, or *Vaitarani*, is a sacred river described in the *Garuda Purana* and other Hindu scriptures. It flows between the earthly realm and *Naraka*, the infernal world ruled by *Yama*, the god of death. The river is believed to cleanse sins—appearing as nectar to the righteous, and as blood to the sinful. Souls must cross it after death, and to aid this passage, a cow is traditionally offered to the *Brahman* priest conducting the funeral rites.

We set out to find a calf and a clergyman, and to my surprise, everything fell into place at once.

Even in the midst of this emotional and complex moment, Kripa, just thirty-two years old, moved with calm resolve. She coordinated with the family, located the priest, and arranged the offering with quiet efficiency. Her understanding of the ritual's meaning, and her ability to act so decisively under pressure, left me deeply moved. I watched her move between guests and tasks—tending to both sacred duties and practical needs—with a grace and depth that made me proud.

As the *Baitarani* ritual concluded, everyone returned to their homes, offering parting words: "If anything happens, please call us."

Kripa's father continued to move around in the same spot, attempting to speak but only producing incomprehensible sounds. It was evident that he was struggling, and the possibility of him being in pain loomed large. Perhaps he had something important to say before his inevitable passing, or maybe he was aware of his impending death and wanted to convey his final wishes. However, the true nature of his thoughts and feelings remained elusive, leaving us to merely speculate on what he was trying to communicate.

Observing him in that state of confusion and distress was heart-wrenching. It was agonizing to witness someone we cared about struggle to express themselves, leaving us feeling helpless in our attempts to understand and provide comfort.

In the background of this heartrending scene, the television broadcast sensational news of the devastating toll of COVID-19, showing images of countless bodies lying out in the open and in hospitals. Some were wrapped in plastic bags and consigned to mass graves. The juxtaposition of Kripa's father's struggle and the grim reality of the pandemic amplified the somber atmosphere, underscoring the fragility and preciousness of life in the face of such a relentless and indiscriminate threat.

Chapter Thirty-Four

Dreams Rest in Seti River

April 6, 2020

My *sasuraba's* movements resembled that of a snail, slow and labored, the simplest motion forward almost beyond his reach. He struggled mightily to make his small circles. His body appeared to be in a state of paralysis, a stark contrast to the active and vibrant person he once was. It was unfathomable how such a drastic change could occur in just twenty-four hours.

I watched him for half an hour as he wrestled to articulate properly. He could barely produce any sound, and when he tried, it resembled nothing more than a feeble tweet, reminiscent of a bird call. The stark contrast between his current state and his former vitality left me in disbelief and filled my heart with profound sorrow. Witnessing him in this condition was both heart-wrenching and surreal, as he grappled with his own physical limitations, and we, as his loved ones, came to terms with the sudden and drastic changes that had befallen him.

"*Buwa*, do you recognize me?" I asked, approaching him and holding his hand gently. But there was no response, no flicker of recognition in his eyes. His entire body had lost its function and purpose. Even the slightest movement was now beyond his grasp. His hands lay motionless, and he no longer was able to crawl. It was devastating to witness him deteriorate so rapidly, losing one ability after another—his voice, senses, mobility, and more. The painful reality was sinking in: he was no longer fighting death and would soon surrender.

In that heart-wrenching moment, I struggled to hold myself together, feeling overwhelmed by the cruel reality unfolding before my eyes. The desperation in my voice betrayed my thoughts as I suggested bringing him to the hospital, clinging to the hope that he could be cured and continue living. But Jaya *dai's* response was a stark reminder of the grim truth of his condition.

Nonetheless, we tried to lift him and transfer him to the bed, hoping to provide some comfort. However, his body had lost its strength and he couldn't hold himself upright, falling back immediately. We surrounded him with pillows, blankets, and anything that could offer support, but nothing seemed to make a difference. He resembled a month-old child, his body limp and helpless, like a jellyfish trying to stand on its own.

The sight was heart-wrenching, and the pain was too much to bear. Kripa and Suman *didi*, seeing their father in such a state, broke down in uncontrollable sobs. The anguish and sorrow enveloped us all as we grappled with the reality of the situation, feeling helpless and distraught in the face of his declining health.

"Why on earth are you all crying again? Please keep quiet," I said, my voice low but controlled, jaw tight. "Get in touch with all the relatives immediately."

Laxman *dai* arrived, and I repeated my naive question, "Can we take him to the hospital?"

"*Jwaisaap*, can't you see his condition?" Laxman *dai* responded, his tone tinged with a hint of sarcasm, "Why would you even think it?"

His words hit me with sudden clarity, and shame crept in as I realized I'd momentarily forgotten the gravity of his condition. My plea felt foolish and out of touch with the reality before us.

At a certain point, I noticed that my father-in-law was in excruciating pain, evident from his strained expressions and faint voice. It seemed like he was attempting to convey his discomfort. It occurred to me that he might benefit from a sip of morphine to alleviate some of his suffering.

Carefully, I soaked the morphine tablet in water and allowed it to dissolve for a few minutes. After mashing it, I gently tried to administer it to him. Some relatives held him securely, while others helped to open his mouth. With my finger, I carefully allowed a few drops to fall into his mouth. Unfortunately, he was unable to swallow, and the liquid dribbled out sideways. The situation was heart-wrenching, and I felt helpless in my attempts to ease his pain.

As the evening progressed, almost all the relatives and neighbors had gathered at the house. Kripa's *fupudidi* kindly offered to take care of Krisha, assuring us that she would look after her during this difficult time. Meanwhile, Zenith and Araju remained by my father-in-law's side, observing the somber atmosphere in the house and offering their support. The presence of our loved ones brought some comfort amidst the turmoil, but the gravity of the situation weighed on us all.

Amidst the fear of COVID-19, even though we all wore facemasks, the looming presence of the pandemic added another layer of dread to the already heart-wrenching situation. While one life was slipping away, the threat of losing someone else to the virus lingered in the air.

"It seems like he's in pain. We should give him morphine," I suggested once again, hoping to alleviate his suffering even a little.

"We tried, but it didn't work," someone in the group replied, their voice filled with helplessness.

Watching him in this condition was agonizing. Some deaths are peaceful, but not this one. Seeing him suffer, I couldn't help but silently wish for death to come swiftly and take him away from his agony. It felt like a cruel thought, but witnessing his distress was unbearable. Some sights are so painful and terrifying that they surpass the fear of death itself.

It was three in the afternoon, and my father-in-law's breathing continued, making him appear like a lifeless log ready for the pyre. Helpless, I could only wish for a swift release from his suffering. He resembled a wounded bird, wings motionless, on the verge of its final breath. In the face of death and disease, we humans are rendered powerless and insignificant.

At that moment, the thought of euthanasia crept into my mind—not out of cruelty, but out of helplessness. I wondered what it meant to ease someone's pain when medicine could no longer help. The idea scared me. But it also made me question what love looks like at the edge of life.

In Nepal, discussions of a euthanasia law had begun, and some doctors, like the renowned neurosurgeon Basanta Pant, have emphasized the need for it. Reflecting on this, I considered whether such a law could bring relief to individuals facing unbearable suffering.

"Let's call the doctor, please!" Kripa shouted, urging us to seek medical help in the midst of our turmoil and contemplation.

In an attempt to offer some comfort, Jaya *dai* called a nearby physician from the pharmacy. However, it seemed almost comical for the doctor, equipped with only a stethoscope, to address the grave situation of an oncology patient. Nonetheless, his presence was meant to console the grieving daughters, who were crying and in distress.

As the health professional measured my father-in-law's blood pressure, I held his hand, feeling its coldness and lack of vitality. The initial reading was already dangerously low at 80/30, as if he had relinquished his fight for life. One minute later, it was measured again, and I continued holding his hand. Suddenly, with a deep, long breath, he passed away, and his blood pressure dropped to 0/0. His once vibrant life was gone. He had departed right before my eyes, as I clutched his hand. In that moment, he transformed into a deceased entity, completely absent from this world.

The room fell into an eerie silence as we all processed the reality of his passing. Kripa and Suman *didi*, having to deal with their father's condition and the loss of their mother, found it challenging to accept their father's demise. As the realization settled in, they rushed to his body and embraced him tightly, overcome with grief and sorrow.

"Please save my father. Isn't there anyone who can help him? Why have both our parents left us? Is there no God? Has God also died? Please, come and rescue him," they cried out, their desperate pleas echoing through the room.

The pain and anguish were unbearable—grief searching for something to hold onto. In their cries, I heard a raw reckoning with life's unfairness, a questioning of everything sacred in the face of profound loss.

Their words brought to mind the verses of Lekhanath Paudyal, the revered Nepali poet:

Bhāka bhul, dayā, kṣamatā ra māmatā, Santaṣa jandaina tyō; Indrai binti garnu jhukera padmā, Kyai binti māndaina tyō. Rājā, ranka sabai samān usakā, Baisamya gardaina tyō; Āyo, ṭappa ṭipyō, lāgyō, miti pugyō—Tārer tārdaina tyō.

Translation: Death listens to neither voice, nor mercy, nor compassion, nor restraint.

Even a bowed plea at Indra's feet will not move it.

For death, king and beggar are the same—it makes no distinction.

It comes, taps your shoulder, and when your time has come, it takes you.

Nothing can stop it.

***

As evening fell, there was a sense of urgency to perform the last rites, but in Nepali culture, it is customary to wait for important people or immediate family members to arrive before cremating the body. Nevertheless, we do not wait for long, and if no significant arrivals are expected, the ceremony takes place without delay. In my heart, I wished for a prompt cremation, so my wife wouldn't have to witness her father's lifeless form and endure additional anguish.

Some in the group discussed the practicalities of finding firewood and other necessities for the process. However, with the evening already upon us, Laxman *dai* proposed waiting until the next morning to complete all the preparations. The night dragged on, and we gathered around the body while Kripa and Suman *didi* sobbed and wailed, their hearts burdened by grief. Kripa's *fupudidi* took care of Krisha during this heartbreaking time, though she was deeply saddened by the loss of her only brother among six siblings. The decision was made to cremate him at the same place where his beloved wife had been cremated, a final tribute to their inseparable bond, even in death.

***

In the morning, a solemn gathering assembled, and Laxman *dai* led the way. We all wore face masks, and I kept a small bottle of sanitizer in my pocket as a precaution. The villagers carried the deceased on a sturdy bamboo stretcher, and together we walked the three miles to the Seti River, where the death ritual would take place. Kripa and Suman *didi* followed the procession, their tearful eyes expressing the immense pain and sorrow in their hearts. The final farewell was heartbreaking, and the sight of their father's lifeless body atop the pyre was profoundly painful.

The daughters had now lost both their parents within a span of just five months. Once the cremation was completed, we returned home, and Kripa and Suman *didi* entered a period of mourning, secluded from the outside world for another thirteen days as per the rituals.

Outside the house, life went on unchanged—the familiar street and temple with its bells tolling, oblivious to the tragedy that had unfolded. The rhythm of life continued as usual for others, unaffected by the loss that had befallen Kripa's family. Yet for Kripa and Suman, their lives had forever been altered. Though they had their own families to care for in the future, the memories of their parents would linger like a gentle whisper in the recesses of their minds until their last breaths.

As we returned home, a sparrow perched on a wire that my father-in-law used to show Krisha, as if to deliver a poignant message. The sparrow flew into the house and settled in a corner of my father-in-law's bedroom. In that moment, I couldn't help but wonder if it was his immortal soul, returning to the familiar surroundings he once cherished, reminding us of the everlasting bond that death could not sever.

Chapter Thirty-Five

Unfulfilled Dreams

May 11, 2018

My *sasuraba* sat on the familiar red couch, watching TV with a contented smile. In his hand, he held the remote, switching between channels, briefly pausing on folk songs and dances before settling on the morning news.

"You are my favorite son-in-law," he said, patting the space beside him. "Come sit next to me and let's chat."

The invitation was met with quiet warmth.

I moved in close, settling cross-legged beside him just as he'd asked.

His breath was shallow, and he shifted carefully to make space.

Our postures matched—close, casual, familiar.

There was comfort in that small nearness, in being exactly where he wanted me to be.

"One day, you and I have to go out without telling anyone in the house and enjoy life to the fullest," he shared this wish with me as he had before, a wide grin on his face, revealing teeth darkened by years of tobacco use. "I'll take you to my favorite spot, where it'll be just the two of us, a bottle of whiskey, some deer meat, and no one else around. But first, let me get well."

"That sounds like a plan, *Buwa*," I replied, using the affectionate term for father-in-law in our region. "I'd love to do that with you."

"Let me revive my health first. I don't know why I get stomach pains sometimes, and the doctors can't seem to diagnose it precisely. I'm sure it's nothing" he said, belief flickering in his eyes. "Once I'm on the mend, we'll head out for that adventure."

"I hope you feel well soon," I said, my voice soft with optimism.

"I will. It's just a minor thing. When you're alive, you experience some pain from time to time," he remarked, calling out to his wife in the kitchen. "Hey Gita, when will the tea be ready? *Jwai* and I are waiting for it. Why are you taking so long?"

Shortly, my *sasuma* brought two cups of milk tea, and we took them from the plate, engaging in conversation while sipping and watching the news on TV. The sun began to rise, casting its warm rays through the window, and I got up and drew the curtains to keep the brightness at bay.

"*Jwaisaap*, I'm so happy to have you as my daughter's husband," he said, looking into my eyes. "I don't know what she first saw in you, but now I see how humble you are."

"Thank you, *Buwa*," I replied, accepting the compliment graciously. "I'm doing my best, and your words inspire me to be even more responsible."

"*Jwaisaap*, it's your time now. You have a long way to go," he said, finishing his tea and setting the glass aside. "You'll have kids, and your responsibilities will multiply. Money isn't everything, but it is essential. Without it, you won't be able to keep your wife happy. Always remember that."

A silent nod acknowledged his advice, the last sip of tea warming my throat as it went down.

"Family is the most important and intimate part of our lives. If we fail to manage it well, everything else will fall apart," he continued, sharing his wisdom with sincerity. "So always work in the best interest of your family; that will maintain happiness forever."

I listened intently, cherishing each word he offered.

The day passed swiftly, steeped in my *sasuraba's* wisdom and stories—gifts from a life well lived.

It was a day I would carry with me always, tucked into memory like something sacred.

A day that deepened the quiet bond between a father-in-law and the son-in-law who would one day tell his story.

Chapter Thirty-Six

Reflection on Death

April 19, 2020

The thirteen days of mourning had passed. So had the Nepali New Year—seven quiet days into 2077.

The year before, 2076, had carried so much death. Kripa's parents. My grandmother. Friends. Strangers. Names whispered through phone lines, across cities, in grief-soaked silence.

All over the world, the virus moved without mercy. Thousands of dead, then millions. In America alone, over 400,000 lost.

Vaccines were on the way, we were told. But for many, they would come too late.

I found myself thinking about death often—not in fear, but in awe of its reach. It touched everything: kings and beggars, insects and elephants, light and shadow. Death entered every space, even the ones the sun forgot.

It was not a question of *if*, only *when*.

And even for those who had walked beside death before, acceptance never came easily.

Strength of body meant nothing. What mattered was a strong heart.

William Blake wrote, *"We have two births in life: one when we are born, and the other when we die."*

To come into existence is to be certain of death.

To die is to be born again—into something we cannot yet know.

In Hindu scripture, we know that death means rebirth. After the person dies, depending on his deeds, he will either go to Heaven or Hell.

Bijayakumar compared death to a hidden watch—not worn on the wrist, but in the heart. A reminder of time. Of duty. A quiet ticking no one else hears.

So many thinkers have tried to shape death with language. Tagore welcomed it as a companion. Nietzsche called pain the pulse of real life. Georges Bataille described death as *"the symbol of life, the way to infinity."*

Even Jimi Hendrix said no one could die in his place—so no one should tell him how to live.

And the Mahabharata speaks plainly: *Death is the architect and destroyer of all things, extinguishing life's flame and crafting both beauty and ruin, only to undo them again.*

Even the gods are not exempt.

Still, we resist.

We fear it, though we know it will come.

We flee from it, though it walks beside us.

Tekendra Adhikari wrote that we run from death because of fear, yes—but also because we've lost touch with nature, with stillness, with the humility that comes from knowing we are not in control.

Emotions like love, greed, anger, and longing complicate that understanding.

But death does not wait for clarity.

It came for Queen Elizabeth.

It came for my wife's parents.

And one day, it will come for us too. The only question is when.

Grief has a way of stripping us bare. We forget who we are.

We stop being subjects of our story and become objects—carried, pushed, undone. But to feel that pain fully, to remain awake within it, is also to be fully alive.

Gitanjali Shree, in *Tomb of Sand*, captured it best through her eighty-year-old protagonist who, after sinking into depression, rises again: *"One can mourn, but what is gone is gone."*

Even Hans Christian Andersen knew: *"Living is not enough... one must have sunshine, freedom, and a little flower."*

So, we mourn. And we live.

We find meaning where we can.

In a song. In a small hand reaching for ours.

In the ache of missing someone whose voice we'll never hear again.

And we whisper to one another, as the evening turns to night:

"Kehi mitho bata gara, raat taisai dhalkidai chha ..."

(Please say something kind, as night begins to fall.

Soon, we will all be alone with our sorrow.)

Chapter Thirty-Seven

Imageries

April 20, 2020

In the morning, Kripa, Krisha, and I went to the top floor of my in-law's house. Jaya *dai*, Suman *didi*, and their children were still sleeping. The garden Kripa's mother had planted a few months ago was green, and the tendrils of bitter gourd, squash, and tomatoes were extending and climbing up the wall. The plants were loaded with vegetables—cauliflower, tomatoes, beans, and others.

Krisha started to play with the tendrils.

I looked to the north and saw the snow-clad *Machhapuchhre* and *Annapurna* mountains, glittering like gold as soon as the first rays of the morning sun fell upon them. The sky was clear, and the hills in the north stretched beyond the horizon—verdant and beautiful. They were untouched by the pandemic, unfazed by the death of my in-laws. In that moment, I wished I could die while gazing at the hills of my own country. I wasn't sure that dream would ever come true. Time would tell.

"My mother tended to this garden, *Budho*," Kripa said, showing me the greens and fruits and vegetables. Her eyes looked damp. "She planted them and always came and watered them. How beautiful it would be if my mother was here. Our days of happiness had just started after my marriage with you, but death took her away."

At a loss for words, I didn't know how to respond to her grief. Tears welled in my own eyes.

Without speaking, we came downstairs to the living room.

Jaya *dai* and Suman *didi* had already awakened; in the kitchen, Suman *didi* moved quietly, making tea.

The house carried on as if nothing had changed—chores beginning, water boiling—but outside, the world had shifted. The lockdown had turned life inside out.

News drifted in through television screens, radios, and online headlines—crime rates had fallen, but the darkest crimes had moved indoors.

Women and children no longer felt safe in their own homes.

In just twenty-one days of lockdown, police had recorded eighty-six cases of rape and seventy-two incidents of domestic violence. Most of the victims were children—assaulted not by strangers, but by those meant to protect them.

Six new reports every day.

Relatives. Neighbors.

Behind locked doors, in the very places meant to shelter them.

It was hard to reconcile these quiet morning motions—tea steeping, slippers on tile—with the weight of what was happening around us.

The world was unraveling at the edges.

And yet somehow, it kept spinning.

Sitting on the faded red couch once cherished by my *sasuraba*, Kripa's father, I found myself immersed in memories of my beloved in-laws. Absentmindedly scrolling through my Facebook feed, I stumbled upon Kripa's poignant post, a poetic tribute to her departed mother.

The garden you looked after on the top floor
Is still the same as it was the day before you left, but
You are gone, mother.
Green are the plants loaded with tomatoes
Cauliflowers, green beans, chilies…
Every morning you watered them, and now
The tulsi, the basil plant is green and exhaling oxygen
But you are gone.
Why is it that the garden you looked after
Couldn't look after you?
Why couldn't the basil plant you gave life
save you when you needed oxygen?
You were as beautiful as the garden—
Lovely, simple, alive, patient, and verdant,
But death kissed you so strongly that it killed you.
Now the laments of hatchlings in a nest
Remain with me after you are gone,
And all that is left for me is this garden so I can behold and
Behold the hills and mountains to the north

Where I see your face smiling, looking at me.
I see your face in every green leaf,
And silently acknowledge, with tear-filled eyes,
The importance of you, the importance of a mother.

After reading her poignant Facebook post, tears welled and cascaded uncontrollably down my cheeks. I could imagine the deep impact her parents had on her, but their passing also awakened her to the profound significance of motherhood and fatherhood, as well as the role and responsibility she now carried for Krisha. My heart swelled with pride as I admired her unique perspective on life. As I continued scrolling through Facebook, another one of her statuses caught my eye.

"One devastating blow after another from the loss of our guardians has not weakened us, but rather made us stronger. I understand that no one can truly fill the void left by our parents, but we must forge ahead and embrace the life that remains for us. I will uphold the values they instilled in us and pass them on to our children. One day, we too will depart this world. Only those who have witnessed it know the true weight of losing both a father and a mother within a span of five months. These heart-wrenching experiences have bestowed upon me valuable lessons, accelerated my maturity, and equipped me to overcome any future obstacles."

A smile formed on my lips as I marveled at how my wife had transformed tragedy into a wellspring of creativity, harnessing the depths of sorrow to cultivate her own inner strength.

Chapter Thirty-Eight

Rites

May 10, 2022

Two years after Kripa bade farewell to her parents, she penned a heartfelt article titled "This Is How I Performed the Rites of My Parents," which found its way to an online news portal. With a mix of emotions, she decided to share this profound piece on her Facebook page, allowing her friends and loved ones a glimpse into her journey.

With her gracious permission, I present her heartfelt words below:

This is how I did my Parents' *Shradda*—**the yearly rites of my parents' death …**

In life, we often encounter unforeseen and abrupt incidents—the kind that leave an indelible mark on our souls. I, too, experienced such a tragic and unforgettable event. I lost both my parents, just five months apart. It was a devastating blow—one that shattered my world.

My mother, who was fifty-three years old, passed away first, leaving us all in shock. She had never been sick before, and her sudden departure was a heart-wrenching ordeal. It happened while we were focused on my father's health. He had been unwell, and we were on our way to seek medical treatment for him when my mother suffered a fatal heart attack.

Witnessing my parents' funerals remains etched in my memory like scenes from a surreal movie. Their bodies turned to ashes, vanishing into thin air, leaving me feeling numb and lost. They were my pillars of strength—the sky and earth that anchored my life. Losing them both in such a short span was an immeasurable pain, and I felt utterly helpless, unable to save either my sky or my earth.

Growing up as their youngest daughter, I was raised more like a son in the family. Despite facing hardships, they showered me with unconditional love and affection, treating me like their precious princess. I will forever cherish those memories and the warmth they bestowed upon me.

The passing of my mother has been especially difficult to accept. It is hard to fathom that just the day before her departure, she had lovingly video-called me before bed. Her sudden absence leaves an emptiness that refuses to be filled. I find it challenging to come to terms with the fact that she left us so soon, breaking the promise of seeing me the next day.

Amidst our sorrowful wails for the loss of our beloved parents, my sister Suman and I were led to the crematorium to perform the solemn ritual of giving dagbatti. Our immediate family members and cousins came forward to support us, expressing their grief by shaving their heads and donning white attire in mourning. The priest insisted that a male member of the household must take up these responsibilities, as it was believed that only a son could ensure the departed souls' passage to Heaven. However, lacking a brother, the duty fell upon us, the daughters.

The pain of losing our parents was overwhelming, and it left us in a state of numbness and disbelief. Our minds were blank, and we could hardly comprehend the situation, even though our bodies continued to function mechanically. We were too emotionally drained to argue with the priest or voice any objections. Returning home after the cremation, we remained quiet and almost unconscious, consumed by the grief that enveloped us.

For the next thirteen days, we observed the mourning rituals, draping *saris* above our buttocks and leaving our hair uncombed. We secluded ourselves in a room, trying to come to terms with the immense loss we had endured.

The priest had decreed that daughters need only mourn in seclusion for five days, even though we continued to eat unsalted food until the thirteenth day. However, due to my responsibility as a breastfeeding mother, they allowed me to finish grieving after five days. It was believed that if the sorrowing was extended for an extended period instead of being performed by a son, it might affect the peaceful rest of our departed parents in Heaven. Sadly, even some women in our community supported this notion.

We were deeply hurt by these customs and beliefs. Our parents' lives had been full of love and care for us, and we could never fathom causing them any difficulty, even after their passing. Nevertheless, societal norms and religious convictions compelled us to abide by these practices. I mourned for five days in seclusion, while my sister continued for the full thirteen days, following the prevailing customs.

The thirteen days of mourning had passed, and our cousins, the sons of my father's brother, had returned to their regular lives. As the anniversary of our parents' death approached, we requested them to perform *Shraddha* on behalf of our beloved departed ones. To our surprise, the priest informed us that this ritual should be conducted annually on their death anniversary. This revelation startled me, and I couldn't help but wonder how long I could rely on my cousins to fulfill this responsibility. The thought of finding someone new each year to carry out *Shraddha* filled me with sorrow.

I questioned the validity of this tradition. Shouldn't the children of the deceased be allowed to conduct *Shraddha* for their own parents? Wouldn't it be a betrayal if I, their daughter, didn't pay tribute to the very ones who gave me life, just as any son would do? I contemplated this issue countless times, feeling that my heart couldn't accept the idea of depending on my cousins. While it might be acceptable for a son to fulfill *Shraddha* even if he's not at his best, why couldn't it be deemed appropriate for a daughter to carry out the rituals with utmost sincerity and devotion?

Seeking guidance, I consulted some elderly members of our society, hoping for a different perspective. However, they too rejected the idea of a female offspring performing *Shraddha*. They firmly believed that only sons could ensure their parents' happiness in the afterlife. According to them, if daughters performed the rituals, the deceased wouldn't find successful passage in the afterlife.

These views hurt me deeply, as I knew how fully my parents cared for me. They shared in my blissfulness and were always there to support me with genuine love and affection. I recalled how they cherished the small gestures of joy I brought into their lives, like celebrating their birthdays with a cake, making them the happiest people in the world. How could I assume that performing *Shraddha* for them every year wouldn't bring them contentment?

Throughout the night, I pondered this dilemma from various angles. I remembered how my mother used to glow with happiness when I gifted her a *Kurta suruwal*, and I wondered why offering something to the less fortunate in their name would make them unhappy. After all, no one has returned from the afterlife to describe Heaven or Hell. So, why must I blindly follow the beliefs of those in society who prioritize sons in the matter of performing *Shraddha*?

The idea that I, as a daughter, cannot fulfill my duty to my parents simply because of what some people said went against my core beliefs. Aren't we, the children, bound by the duty of love and respect for them? Should our responsibilities end once we get married and move to our husband's homes? These thoughts created a storm in my mind. Ultimately,

I resolved that even though I couldn't serve like a son, and my offerings might not be exactly the same, I would perform *Shraddha* every year with all the love and devotion in my heart.

On the day of my parents' death anniversary, I arrived at the sacred Pashupatinath Temple early in the morning. A row of priests sat in wait, and I came prepared with all the necessary items for the *Shraddha* ritual, thanks to the help of my husband who accompanied me to the market.

Approaching one of the priests, I placed my hands together and bowed slightly before speaking. "*Guru*, my parents raised me and my sister like sons in our family. They empowered and supported us just as they would a son. Through their hard work at the restaurant, they provided us with an education, enabling us to graduate from college.

Both of them have passed away now, and I wish to perform the rituals after their death just as a son would. I request, with great respect, that you do not let the ritual fall short in any way."

The priest looked at me with surprise, his expression softening with appreciation.

"Your parents must be truly grateful to have a daughter like you. Having a daughter like you will undoubtedly bring them happiness in Heaven. I will do my utmost to perform all the specific rituals that a son would do. Please sit down, and I will begin the *Pinda dan* ceremony."

I settled down and attentively followed the priest's instructions. I crafted the *Pinda*, offered water by the bank of the Bagmati River, and gently released the *Pinda* into the water, praying for the peaceful rest of my parents and all departed souls. Facing the four directions, I reverently poured water from the Bagmati River with cupped hands.

A sense of relief and contentment washed over me. As the ritual drew to a close, I once again cupped the sacred Bagmati water, directing my gaze toward the towering pole *gajur* of the Pashupatinath Temple. With a heartfelt gesture, I poured the water from above my head. In that moment, I imagined the radiant smiles of my parents, seated atop the temple, expressing their satisfaction and happiness with the *Shraddha* ceremony I had performed. This vision filled my heart with gratitude and peace.

In the eyes of the priest, and more importantly, in the eyes of my parents, I had done justice to the rituals of *Shraddha*, transcending the conventional boundaries that limited such practices to sons. For me, it was a profound revelation that the love and devotion with which I conducted the ceremony mattered far more than societal norms. I left the temple with a deep sense of fulfillment, knowing that the love I offered in tribute to my parents' memories would forever transcend any cultural or traditional constraints.

Chapter Thirty-Nine

Death: Lessons

April 21, 2020

The thirteen days of mourning had passed, but the weight of loss lingered. And yet, even in the shadow of death, life pressed forward. Somehow, as I watched one life ending, I noticed another beginning.

Grief and grace shared the same breath.

Amid the sorrow, I began to understand that sadness didn't stand alone. There was joy within it. There was unity.

Laughter cracked open between tears, and family—scattered by time and distance—had come together again, drawn into each other's arms by grief.

Is death always a curse? Or could it, somehow, also be a blessing?

On the thirteenth day, the house filled with voices—relatives, neighbors, old friends.

I introduced myself again and again, not just as a son-in-law, but as part of something larger.

Some relatives embraced me warmly, saying, "Don't forget us. You're one of us now."

That day reminded me: death doesn't only take.

Sometimes, it gives.

It carves space for reconnection, for tenderness, for truths we overlook in the rush of living.

Still, not everything could be healed.

As we lit the final lamps, a quiet ache lingered—knowing Krisha would never remember the embrace of her grandparents.

That kind of absence settles deep, beyond words.

In those weeks, I returned often to the books I had once loved—poems, philosophy, stories of others who had walked through grief. Writers like

Eliot and Tagore, Kalanithi and Nabokov, tried in their own ways to make peace with death.

Some saw it as a companion, others as a teacher.

But none of them ever made it less mysterious.

What they did offer—what I clung to—was the reminder that death, like life, demands relationship.

To face it alone is terrifying.

But to face it with a hand in yours, with no words left unspoken, with devotion offered freely—that is how love gives meaning to loss.

The passing of Kripa's parents changed me.

I loved them already, but losing them taught me to adore them more deeply, to honor them not just in ritual, but in the way I show up for their daughter and granddaughter.

At first, I feared Kripa might collapse under the grief.

Her cries were sharper than I'd ever heard—even sharper, she once said, than the pain of labor.

And I feared I wouldn't be enough for her. That I'd fail her and Krisha both.

But time did its quiet work.

One morning, Kripa woke early, wrapped her arms around me, and whispered.

"*Budho*, maybe my parents are sleeping together in Heaven. Just like I'm hugging you now."

I looked into her eyes, pulled her close, and said, "Perhaps, my love."

I didn't need to believe in Heaven to believe in that moment.

In my heart, I imagined them somewhere peaceful—together again, their love and labor remembered, their kindness still echoing in the stories that others had shared.

They had given so much. I would carry their memory by giving what I could in return.

One thing my *sasuraba* said had stayed with me: "The most important thing is the happiness of your family."

With Krisha asleep beside us and Kripa's arms around me, I understood.

This was the lesson.

Not one of death, but of life:

To cherish.

To comfort.

To remember.

And to keep loving, while we can.

The World Beyond the Page

This section offers curated reflections and expanded insights into the cultural, emotional, and philosophical landscapes that shape the memoir. Organized thematically, contextual notes and referenced sources invite readers to explore the deeper world that lives beyond the events on the page.

I. Cultural & Social Commentary

The Cost of a Cup of Tea
In Nepal, the price of a cup of tea can tell you more than an economic report. It reveals the stark contrast between locals and tourists, between survival and comfort. For some, the comforting drink is a daily necessity shared in tin or glass cups; for others, it's a luxury steeped in imported spices and served in fine china. These contrasts remind us that every rupee spent carries social and cultural meaning—and for many Nepalis, survival means constantly measuring the cost of the ordinary.

Inheritance, Daughters, and Patriarchy
In traditional Nepali society, sons inherit the land, the home, and the honor of the family name. Daughters, beloved but often undervalued, are raised to leave. This entry explores how cultural expectations, religious teachings, and legal systems combine to create generational patterns where women must fight for their rightful place—economically, emotionally, and socially.

From the Villages to the Capital
Kathmandu stands like a mirage to many villagers: a place of opportunity, escape, and promise. But for countless migrants, the city offers harsh realities—overcrowding, exploitation, and disillusionment. This reflection examines the gap between rural hope and urban reality, and the ways dreams bend under the weight of survival.

Bhanubhakta Acharya and Nepali Identity
Bhanubhakta Acharya is more than a poet; he is a symbol of linguistic unity and cultural pride. His translation of the Ramayana into Nepali helped define a national identity. This entry explores how literary figures like him continue to shape consciousness and why reclaiming one's language can feel like reclaiming one's soul.

Luxury Hotels and Everyday Life
Tourists who visit Nepal might never see the narrow alleys behind their hotel courtyards—the ones where locals cook over firewood and wash clothes in plastic tubs. This contrast highlights the dual economies and the ways in which visibility, comfort, and currency can shield one world from the reality of another.

II. Emotional & Philosophical Reflections

On Mind Blanking and Emotional Overload
During moments of acute stress—like rushing to the airport with my grieving wife and infant daughter—I experienced what psychologists Adrian F. Ward and Daniel M. Wegner call "mind blanking," where "the mind seems to disappear... and there are times when it is actually gone." In the moment, it felt like an internal switch had flipped. Thoughts vanished. Emotions stalled. There was only movement, breath, and the sound of my heart pounding. I wouldn't have had the words for it then, but the experience is etched into my memory. It taught me how grief, fear, and urgency can silence even the inner voice.

The Distance Between Us: Reflections on Fatherhood, Absence, and Cultural Expectations
The emotional cost of absence—especially for parents navigating caregiving obligations abroad. Drawing from cultural teachings and personal guilt, reflect on:
- The weight of time not given.

- Gendered expectations of caregiving.

- The Gita's silence on parental tenderness.

- The slow reckoning with roles unmet.

The Nature of Hope: A Reflection on What Carries Us
Hope is a powerful force that sustains us in times of uncertainty and adversity. It acts as a beacon, guiding us through the darkest moments and providing the strength to carry on. Even in the face of terminal illness, as I watched someone that I loved fading away, I had to model hope—not because I felt it, but because it was needed. It reminds us that possibilities remain, even when the world closes in. As long as a person breathes, hope endures.

III. Health, Ethics & Global Perspectives

Attachment Theory
Originally developed by John Bowlby and expanded by Mary Ainsworth, attachment theory explores how early relationships shape emotional development. As summarized by Kendra Cherry (2022), secure attachments lead to better emotional regulation, while inconsistent caregiving can result in insecurity and low self-esteem. Though often centered on mothers, this theory also calls attention to fathers—their presence or absence, and the silent weight it carries.

Patient Rights Across Borders: Ethical Tensions in Disclosure
In the U.S., the Patient's Bill of Rights ensures that individuals are fully informed of their diagnoses. In Nepal, such disclosure is often filtered through family members or hidden completely. This entry compares the ethical frameworks behind patient autonomy and medical paternalism, and how navigating these systems reveals both cultural loyalty and internal conflict.

Public Figures and Pancreatic Cancer: Stories That Inspired Hope
Ruth Bader Ginsburg and Alex Trebek were more than public figures—they were warriors who fought pancreatic cancer in the public eye. Their resilience offered hope to others facing the disease and sparked global awareness. Their legacies live on as reminders that courage in illness can be a form of leadership.

Pancreatic Cancer: Statistics, Risk Factors, and Global Disparities
Pancreatic cancer ranks seventh in global cancer-related deaths. In Nepal, 229 deaths were reported in 2017, placing the country 156th glob-

ally (WHO data). By contrast, the U.S. had over 56,000 diagnosed cases in 2020. Risk factors include smoking, obesity, diabetes, and chronic pancreatitis. As Rawla et al. (2019) note: the burden is higher in developed nations, but its toll is universal.

Understanding Euthanasia: Definitions and Global Context
Derived from Greek, "euthanasia" means "good death." It refers to intentionally ending life to alleviate suffering. Legal distinctions vary:
- Voluntary: with patient's consent (legal in Netherlands, Belgium)
- Non-voluntary: no consent available (rare and heavily regulated)
- Involuntary: against the patient's will (illegal globally) This reflection explores how moral frameworks, legality, and love collide in moments of impossible decision.

IV. The Pandemic in Context

Timeline of the COVID-19 Outbreak in Nepal
- January 5, 2020: First COVID-related death in Nepal
- January 23, 2020: Over 600 infected and 25 dead
- Lockdowns implemented globally, including Wuhan
- Preventative protocols: handwashing, distancing, masks This snapshot captures the early wave of fear and the slow-motion impact of a global crisis.

COVID-19: Early Global Impact and Nepal's Lockdown
As the virus spread, Nepal went into lockdown. Across the globe, deaths climbed—in Wuhan, Italy, India, and the U.S. Political narratives sharpened, with U.S. President Donald Trump calling it the "China Virus." In Nepal, the economic fallout was swift. Unemployment led many to return to their villages by foot. Suicide rates rose. Within families, even hugs were suspended. We had masked ourselves, not only against illness, but against despair.

The World Beyond the Page invites you to dwell in these layered realities—to sit with discomfort, contradiction, beauty, and truth. These stories are not only told. They are lived, remembered, and now, shared.

References

American Cancer Society. "Marijuana and Cancer." Accessed 2022. https://www.cancer.org/treatment/treatments-and-side-effects/complementary-and-alternative-medicine/marijuana-and-cancer.html.

American Medical Association. "Patient Rights: Code of Medical Ethics Opinion 1.1.3." Accessed 2022. https://www.ama-assn.org/delivering-care/ethics/patient-rights.

Bhatta, L. "Pradeep Giri's Lockdown Diary: Death Is True, Why Fear?" *RatoPati*, April 1, 2020. https://ratopati.com/story/124282/2020/4/1/pradeep-giri-corona-virus-crisis.

Bijaya Kumar. *Sambandhharu*. Kathmandu: Fine Print, 2020.

Cancer.net. "Cancer.Net." Accessed 2022. https://www.cancer.net/.

Cherry, Kendra. "What Is Attachment Theory? The Importance of Early Emotional Bonds." *Verywell Mind*, 2022. https://www.verywellmind.com/what-is-attachment-theory-2795337.

Hamrobazar. "CBD Oil." Accessed 2022. https://hamrobazaar.com.

K.C., Nawaraj. *Sunyako Mulya*. Kathmandu: Shangrila, 2022.

Kafle, D. "Dignified Death." *The Kathmandu Post*, June 1, 2020. https://kathmandupost.com/columns/2020/06/01/the-banality-of-death.

Koirala, Dhundiraj. *Mahabharat Katha*. Kathmandu: Manjari Publication, 2017.

Liveraga, J. A. "A New Philosophy of Life and Death." *New Acropolis Library*, 2016. https://library.acropolis.org/a-new-philosophy-of-life-and-death/.

Mainali, N. "86 Rapes, 72 Domestic Violence Cases in 21 Days of Lockdown." *Naya Patrika*, April 20, 2020. https://www.nayapatrikadaily.com/news-details/41628/2020-04-20.

Mayo Clinic. "Chemotherapy." Accessed 2022. https://www.mayoclinic.org/tests-procedures/chemotherapy/about/pac-20385033.

Pandey, K. R., B. K. C., and K. Tobin. "Epiphanies from Death Park: Insights on Life, Death, and Beyond." In *Educating for Life and Death*, edited by K. Tobin and K. Alexakos. Leiden: Brill, 2023.

Raj, Y. *Sandhya Samrachana*. Kathmandu: Martin Chautari, 2013.

Rawla, P., S. Tagore, and V. Gaduputi. "Epidemiology of Pancreatic Cancer: Global Trends, Etiology and Risk Factors." *World Journal of Oncology* 10, no. 1 (2019): 10–27. https://doi.org/10.14740/wjon1166.

Rimé, Bernard. "Emotion Elicits the Social Sharing of Emotion: Theory and Empirical Review." *Emotion Review* 1 (2009): 60–65.

Sapkota, J. "40 Incidents of Rape during Lockdown." *Kantipur*, April 13, 2020. https://ekantipur.com/news/2020/04/13/158674806088538721.html.

Schneider, B. H., et al. "Child-Parent Attachment and Children's Peer Relations: A Quantitative Review." *Developmental Psychology* 37, no. 1 (2001): 86–100.

Shree, Geetanjali. *Tomb of Sand*. Translated by Daisy Rockwell. London: Tilted Axis Press, 2022.

WebMD. "Medical Marijuana and Cancer." Accessed 2022. https://www.webmd.com/cancer/medical-marijuana-cancer.

Wikipedia. "Alex Trebek." Accessed 2022. https://en.wikipedia.org/wiki/Alex_Trebek.

———. "List of People Diagnosed with Pancreatic Cancer." Accessed 2022. https://en.wikipedia.org/wiki/List_of_people_diagnosed_with_pancreatic_cancer.

———. "Ruth Bader Ginsburg." Accessed 2022. https://en.wikipedia.org/wiki/Ruth_Bader_Ginsburg.

World Health Organization (WHO). "Palliative Care." Accessed 2022. https://www.who.int/news-room/fact-sheets/detail/palliative-care.

World Life Expectancy. "World Health Rankings: Pancreatic Cancer in Nepal." Accessed 2022. https://www.worldlifeexpectancy.com/nepal-pancreas-cancer#:~:text=Nepal%3A%20Pancreas%20Cancer.

Worldometers. "Coronavirus Update." Accessed 2021. https://www.worldometers.info/coronavirus/.

Glossary

Achhuchhuchu (*interj.*) *[ah-choo-choo-choo]*: A Nepali expression used instinctively in response to cold or sudden discomfort, especially when touching icy water. Often repeated in a shivering tone, it conveys a visceral reaction and is culturally rooted in daily Nepali speech.

Annapurna (*n.*) *[uh-nuh-PUR-nuh]*: A massif in the Himalayas of north-central Nepal, named after the Hindu goddess of food and nourishment. The range includes several peaks over 7,000 meters and holds deep spiritual and cultural significance in Nepal.

Anulom Vilom *[uh-noo-lohm vee-lohm]*: A traditional form of alternate nostril breathing in yogic practice, used to calm the mind, balance energy, and promote mental clarity. Practitioners inhale through one nostril while closing the other, then switch nostrils to exhale, repeating the pattern in a slow, rhythmic cycle. In the memoir, Anulom Vilom becomes a rare moment of inner stillness amidst external chaos.

Baba (*n.*) *[BAH-bah]*: A Nepali term for "father," used affectionately by children and within families. It is a common, loving form of address across generations.

Bagbazzar (*n.*) *[BAHG-bah-zar]*: A busy commercial neighborhood in central Kathmandu, known for its medical labs, educational institutions, and markets. Often frequented for healthcare services and administrative errands.

Bagmati River (*n.*): A sacred river flowing through the Kathmandu Valley in Nepal. Considered holy by both Hindus and Buddhists, the Bagmati is closely associated with funeral rites and spiritual cleansing. Temples like Pashupatinath line its banks, where cremation ceremonies are performed and ashes are released into the water to aid in the soul's journey toward liberation.

Baitarani / Vaitarani (*n.*) *[bye-TAH-rah-nee / vy-TAH-rah-nee]*: A sacred river in Hindu mythology, believed to separate the earthly world from *Naraka* (hell). Described in the *Garuda Purana*, it is said that souls must cross this river after death. The righteous see it as flowing with nectar, while the sinful perceive it as blood. A ritual offering of a cow is traditionally made to ensure safe passage for the departed soul.

Belleka roti (*n.*) *[BEHL-leh-kah ROH-tee]*: A traditional Nepali flatbread made from wheat flour, often served warm with yogurt. Simple, hearty, and nourishing, it is a beloved comfort food commonly eaten for breakfast or as a snack.

Bikram Sambat (B.S.) (*n.*) *[BEEK-rahm SAHM-butt]*: The official calendar used in Nepal, which is approximately 56.7 years ahead of the Gregorian calendar. For example, the year 2076 B.S. corresponds to 2019–2020 A.D. The Nepali New Year typically begins in mid-April.

Brahman (*n.*) *[BRAH-muhn]*: A priest belonging to the highest caste in Hindu society, often responsible for conducting religious rituals, including funerals. In the context of the *Baitarani* ritual, a *Brahman* priest receives offerings such as a cow to help guide the soul of the deceased.

Budho (*n., informal*): A Nepali term meaning "old man," often used affectionately between loved ones. In intimate contexts, it serves as a term of endearment, carrying warmth, familiarity, and tenderness rather than referring strictly to age.

Buwa (*n.*) *[BOO-wah]*: A Nepali term meaning "father," commonly used as an affectionate and respectful way to address one's father-in-law in many regions of Nepal. The word reflects emotional closeness and familial respect, especially in spoken conversation.

Chai *[ch-eye]*: A spiced milk tea brewed with black tea leaves, sugar, and often cardamom, ginger, or cloves. In Nepal and India, *chai* is more than a beverage—it's a daily ritual, a social connector, and a comfort. Offered to guests, sipped during roadside conversations, or craved in moments of fatigue, *chai* anchors everyday life with its warmth and familiarity.

Chowk (*n.*) *[chowk]*: A Nepali and South Asian term for a central square, junction, or crossroads in a town or city. A *chowk* is typically a bustling public area where roads meet, often surrounded by shops, tea stalls, vendors, and gathering places. It serves as a hub of daily life and local commerce.

Chowki *[chow-kee]*: A low, wooden platform commonly used in South Asian homes for sitting or sleeping. Often placed directly on the floor, a *chowki* may be topped with a thin mattress or cushion. In many Nepali households, it serves as both a practical piece of furniture and a gathering place for conversation, prayer, or rest. Its simplicity reflects a way of life grounded in modesty, tradition, and closeness to the earth.

Dagbatti (*n.*): A traditional Nepali Hindu ritual in which a close male relative, usually the eldest son, lights the funeral pyre of the deceased. The act symbolizes the release of the soul from the physical body.

Darbar Marga (*n.*) *[DAR-bar MAR-gah]*: Also known as Durbar Marg, this is a prominent boulevard in Kathmandu lined with upscale shops, hotels, and embassies. The name means "Palace Road," as it leads to the historic Royal Palace.

Dashain (*n.*) *[DAH-shine]*: The longest and most widely celebrated Hindu festival in Nepal, lasting fifteen days in autumn. It honors the goddess Durga's victory over evil and is marked by family gatherings, animal sacrifices, blessings from elders, and the placing of *tika* on the forehead as a symbol of protection and prosperity.

Death of the Moth: A brief essay by English writer Virginia Woolf, in which she describes a moth's futile struggle against death after it becomes trapped inside her window. Though small and ordinary, the moth's final moments evoke awe and sympathy, symbolizing the quiet persistence of life—and its inevitable end. In the memoir, this reference echoes the narrator's contemplation of loss and fragility during a time of grief.

Didi *[dee-dee]*: A respectful and affectionate word meaning "older sister" in Nepali and Hindi, often used beyond blood relation. In daily conversation, *didi* can address any woman slightly older, conveying familiarity, warmth, and honor.

Fupudidi (*n.*) *[FOO-poo-dee-dee]*: A respectful and affectionate Nepali term for one's paternal grandfather's sister. Often used to refer to an elder female relative who plays a nurturing or guiding role within the extended family. It reflects both kinship and generational reverence.

Gajur (*n.*): A decorative, often gilded spire or finial atop Nepali temples and stupas, symbolizing spiritual ascent and divine presence. The *gajur* is a prominent architectural feature seen on many Hindu and Buddhist shrines in Nepal.

Garuda Purana (*n.*) *[guh-ROO-dah poo-RAH-nah]*: One of the eighteen *Mahāpurāṇa* texts in Hindu scripture, attributed to Vishnu and his mount, Garuda. It discusses topics such as death, funeral rites, the afterlife, and moral teachings, and is often recited during Hindu mourning rituals in Nepal and India.

Guru (*n.*): In Nepali culture, a respectful term to address Hindu priests or spiritual leaders, especially during religious rituals and ceremonies. The word conveys reverence and is often used when seeking blessings, guidance, or performing rites at temples or sacred sites.

Jute (*n.*) *[joot]*: A coarse, natural fiber derived from the stalks of the jute plant, commonly used in South Asia to make sacks, ropes, and mats. In Nepal, these sacks are a familiar everyday object—rough in texture, often hand-stitched, and used for carrying rice, grains, or vegetables. Describing a body as stitched like a jute sack evokes an image of something patched, worn, and resilient—deeply tied to rural life and labor.

Jwaisaap (*n.*) *[JWHY-sahp]*: A respectful Nepali term to address a son-in-law. The suffix -saap (short for *sahab*) conveys formality and honor, often used by elders as a sign of respect.

Kanchhi (*n.*) *[KAHN-chee]*: A Nepali term of endearment meaning "younger girl" or "youngest daughter," often used affectionately for a younger sister, daughter, or wife. It carries a tone of familiarity, love, and sometimes playfulness within families or close relationships.

Kathmandu (*n.*) *[kaht-man-DOO]*: The capital and largest city of Nepal, located in the Kathmandu Valley at the foothills of the Himalayas. A vibrant cultural, religious, and historical center, Kathmandu is home to ancient temples, bustling markets, and sacred rivers. It serves as the spiritual and political heart of the nation, blending centuries-old traditions with the complexities of modern urban life.

Kilogram (*n.*) *[KIL-oh-gram]*: A metric unit of mass equal to approximately 2.2 pounds. Commonly used in Nepal and most countries outside the United States to measure body weight and food quantities.

Kimkartavyavimudh *[keen-kar-bya-bee-moodh]*: A Sanskrit-derived Nepali term referring to a state of mental paralysis or indecision (much like Hamlet's internal conflict in Shakespeare's play) to describe someone who is momentarily overwhelmed and unsure of how to proceed.

Koteshwor /ko-tesh-wor/: A busy transit and commercial hub in Kathmandu, known for its chaotic intersections and as a transfer point for public transportation. The narrator transfers buses here en route to the hospital.

Kurta suruwal (*n.*): A traditional Nepali outfit for women, consisting of a long tunic-style top (*kurta*) and tapered pants (*suruwal*). Worn in daily life or for special occasions.

Lajjawati jhar (*n.*) *[luh-JAW-wuh-tee jhahr]*: A plant known in English as the touch-me-not or sensitive plant (*Mimosa pudica*), whose leaves fold inward when touched. In Nepali, its name translates to "shame-laden shrub," symbolizing shyness or modesty. Used poetically to describe someone who is gentle or bashful.

Lito *[lee-toh]*: A traditional Nepali porridge made from roasted grain flour, typically prepared for infants or young children. Nutritious and easy to digest, *lito* is often served warm with milk, water, or ghee and is considered a staple weaning food in many Nepali households.

Machhapuchhre (*n.*) *[mah-chhah-POO-chray]*: A sacred mountain in north-central Nepal, its name meaning "Fishtail" in Nepali due to its distinctive double summit. Revered in Hindu culture and considered unclimbable, *Machhapuchhre* is part of the Annapurna range in the Himalayas.

Mahabharata (*n.*) *[mah-hah-BAH-rah-tuh]*: One of the two great ancient Sanskrit epics of Hindu literature, the *Mahabharata* tells the story of a dynastic struggle between the Pandavas and Kauravas and explores themes of duty (*dharma*), justice, war, and the nature of life and death. It contains the *Bhagavad Gita*, a central philosophical text. Revered across South Asia, the epic continues to shape moral, spiritual, and cultural life in Nepal and beyond.

Mahanayak (*n.*) *[mah-HAH-nah-yak]*: A Nepali honorific meaning "great actor" or "superstar," used to refer to iconic figures in film and performing arts. The title is most closely associated with actor Rajesh Hamal.

Mahāpurāṇa (*n.*) *[mah-HAH-poo-RAH-nah]*: A term referring to a group of eighteen major Hindu texts that explore cosmology, mythology, genealogy, ethics, and spiritual teachings. The *Mahāpurāṇas* are considered foundational scriptures in Hinduism and have shaped religious rituals, beliefs, and cultural traditions throughout South Asia, including Nepal.

Maiju (*n.*) *[MY-joo]*: A Nepali familial term referring to one's maternal uncle's wife—essentially, a maternal aunt-in-law. The word carries affection and respect, and in extended family relationships distinguishes her from other types of aunts (*buwaama, fupudidi*, etc.).

Makhamali flower (*n.*) *[muh-khuh-MAA-lee]*: A small, vibrant, globe-shaped flower known scientifically as *Gomphrena globosa*. The Makhamali—especially the deep magenta variety—is beloved in Nepali culture for its longevity and softness. Its name comes from "makhamal," meaning velvet, reflecting the flower's plush texture. Traditionally used to make tika garlands (mala) during Bhai Tika, the final day of the Tihar festival, the Makhamali symbolizes long life, enduring bonds, and sibling devotion.

Mama (*n.*) *[MAH-mah]*: A Nepali term for "mother," widely used by children and family members as an expression of love and closeness. At times, this term is also used to address the maternal uncle.

Namaskar *[nah-mah-SKAR]*: A respectful Nepali greeting, similar to "hello" or "I bow to you," often with elders, professionals, or in formal settings. It conveys both reverence and goodwill.

Namaste *[nah-mah-STAY]*: A traditional salutation in Nepal and many South Asian cultures, spoken with hands pressed together at the heart and a slight bow of the head. The word means "I bow to you" and carries a sense of respect, humility, and spiritual acknowledgment. Used both in greeting and farewell, *Namaste* reflects deep cultural values of honor and interconnectedness.

Naraka (*n.*) *[NAH-rah-kah]*: The Hindu concept of hell or the infernal realm where souls are punished for their sins. Ruled by *Yama*, the god of death, *Naraka* is depicted as a temporary purgatory through which the soul passes before reincarnation or liberation.

Narayan Gopal (*n.*) *[NAH-rah-yahn GO-pahl]*: Widely regarded as the "Swar Samrat" (Emperor of Voice) of Nepal, Narayan Gopal (1939–1990) was a legendary singer and composer known for his soulful, emotional music. His songs, centered on love, longing, and reflection, continue to resonate deeply across generations. A cultural icon, his voice and lyrics have shaped the emotional and musical landscape of modern Nepal.

Nepal (*n.*) *[nuh-PAHL]*: A landlocked country in South Asia, nestled between India and China, known for its diverse geography—from the flat Terai plains to the towering peaks of the Himalayas, including Mount Everest. Rich in cultural heritage, religious traditions, and natural beauty, Nepal is home to numerous ethnic groups, languages, and spiritual practices, including Hinduism and Buddhism. It is the birthplace of the Buddha and a nation where ancient customs continue to shape daily life.

Nepal Yatayat *[nay-pahl yah-tah-yaht]*: A bus service that operates routes within the Kathmandu Valley and beyond. The word *yatayat* means "transportation." In the memoir, it provides a crucial link in the narrator's journey to the teaching hospital.

Palliative care (*n.*) *[PAL-ee-uh-tiv]*: A specialized form of medical care focused on relieving pain and improving quality of life for patients with serious or terminal illnesses. It does not aim to cure the disease, but to provide comfort, manage symptoms, and support emotional and spiritual well-being for both patients and their families.

Paracetamol (*n.*) *[puh-RAH-see-tuh-mawl]*: A common over-the-counter pain reliever and fever reducer, known as acetaminophen in the United States (brand name: Tylenol). Widely used in Nepal and other countries for mild to moderate pain relief.

Pashupatinath Temple (*n.*): One of the most sacred Hindu temples dedicated to Lord Shiva, located on the banks of the Bagmati River in Kathmandu, Nepal. A UNESCO World Heritage Site, it is a major pilgrimage destination, especially significant during death rituals, cremations, and religious festivals such as Maha Shivaratri.

Pinda dan (*n.*): A sacred Hindu ritual performed to honor deceased ancestors, in which offerings of rice balls (*pinda*) are made to help ensure peace and liberation of the departed soul. Often performed by a priest at a temple or sacred site, *pinda dan* is an important part of Nepali funeral and memorial traditions.

Pokhara (*n.*) *[POH-khah-rah]*: A picturesque city in central Nepal, known for its lakes, stunning views of the Annapurna Mountain range, and as a gateway for trekkers in the Himalayas. A popular tourist destination, Pokhara also holds cultural and emotional significance for many Nepali families.

Rajesh Hamal (*n.*) *[rah-JESH HAH-mahl]*: A legendary Nepali film actor known for his roles in action and romantic dramas. Often referred to as the *Mahanayak* (superstar) of Nepali cinema, he has played a major role in shaping the country's film industry since the early 1990s.

Ratnapark *[rut-nuh-park]*: A public park and surrounding area in central Kathmandu, Nepal. Named after Queen Ratna, it has long been a gathering place for political protests, public speeches, and social activity. The park and its surroundings serve as a microcosm of the city's contrasts—offering leisure, internet access, and community while also being home to street vendors, the unemployed, the elderly, and sex workers navigating legal risk. In the memoir, Ratnapark appears as a vibrant, chaotic backdrop to a moment of quiet personal urgency.

Saris (*n.*): Long, draped garments worn by women throughout South Asia, including Nepal. Typically wrapped around the waist and over one shoulder, saris are worn with a blouse and petticoat and may be styled differently for daily wear, special occasions, or mourning rituals.

Sasuma (*n.*) *[SAH-soo-mah]*: A respectful Nepali term for one's mother-in-law, combining *sasu* (mother-in-law) with *ma*, a familiar and affectionate suffix. Used in domestic and emotional contexts to express closeness or reverence.

Sasuraba (*n.*): A title of honor in Nepali referring to one's father-in-law. It combines *sasura* (father-in-law) with *ba* (a suffix meaning "father"), conveying affection, reverence, and familial closeness.

Shraddha (*n.*): A sacred Hindu ceremony performed to honor and pay tribute to deceased ancestors, typically involving offerings and prayers to ensure peace for the departed soul.

Sisuwa (*n.*) *[SEE-soo-wah]*: A village area located in the Kaski District of central Nepal, near Pokhara. Known for its cold climate and frequent winter fog, Sisuwa offers occasional views of the Himalayan peaks, including *Machhapuchhre* and *Annapurna*, though these are often obscured until the sun clears the mist. The village reflects a quiet, rural pace of life with deep ties to natural beauty and mountain culture.

Swar Samrat (*n.*) *[swar SAHM-raht]*: A Nepali honorific meaning "Emperor of Voice," bestowed upon legendary singer Narayan Gopal in recognition of his unmatched vocal mastery and emotional depth. The title reflects his enduring influence on Nepali music and culture.

Tabala *[tuh-buh-luh]*: A pair of traditional Indian and Nepali hand-played drums, known for their intricate rhythms and delicate fingerwork. One drum produces deeper bass sounds, while the other offers higher-pitched tones. Commonly used in classical music, devotional songs, and folk performances, the *tabala* is not just an instrument but an expressive art form, often mimicked playfully in everyday gestures, as when drumming on a steering wheel.

Tamasa *(n.) [tuh-MAA-suh]*: A dramatic display or emotional spectacle, often marked by intense expression, public grief, or theatrical behavior. In South Asian cultures, *tamasa* can imply a chaotic or exaggerated scene—sometimes viewed as overly dramatic, but at other times reflecting real pain that erupts in visible, overwhelming ways. It may carry a tone of disapproval, empathy, or ambivalence, depending on the observer's perspective.

Teaching Hospital: Short for Tribhuvan University Teaching Hospital, a major government-run medical institution in Kathmandu known for both patient care and education. It serves as a referral center and training ground for future doctors. In the memoir, it's where the narrator returns to retrieve a critical report for his father-in-law.

Tika (*n.*) *[TEE-kah]*: A sacred red paste (often mixed with rice and yogurt) applied to the forehead during Hindu rituals and festivals, symbolizing blessing, protection, and the spiritual third eye. During *Dashain*, elders place *tika* on the foreheads of younger family members while offering prayers and blessings.

Tikathali *[tee-kah-thuh-lee]*: A suburban area located in the Lalitpur District of the Kathmandu Valley. Often a residential starting point for travel into central Kathmandu. In the memoir, Tikathali is where the narrator begins his journey to retrieve medical documents.

Trishuli River (*n.*) *[TRIH-shoo-lee]*: A major river in central Nepal, originating from the Langtang region and named after the *trishul* (trident) of the Hindu god Shiva. Known for its powerful current, winding path through deep gorges, and significance to both travelers and pilgrims, the Trishuli River is a vital natural artery. It is also infamous for accidents along its adjoining roads, making it a symbol of both beauty and danger in Nepal's landscape.

Yama (*n.*) *[YAH-mah]*: The Hindu god of death and ruler of *Naraka*. Yama is considered the cosmic judge who determines the fate of souls after death, weighing their karma to assign reward or punishment.

Acknowledgements

This book could not have come into being without the encouragement, guidance, and love of many people.

First, I owe deep gratitude to my family—my parents, my wife Kripa, and my daughters Krisha and Kirtan—whose patience and support carried me through the long seasons of writing, revising, and remembering. Your belief in me has been my constant source of strength.

I am grateful to **Dr. Kay Traille** for her steadfast encouragement. To my teacher and mentor, **Tony Grooms, Georgia Writers Hall of Fame inductee**, thank you for your example of excellence, your generous spirit, and for reminding me that stories carry the power to heal and connect us. I am thankful to **Chika Unigwe, award-winning international author**, whose guidance inspired me to write, revise, and persist. I also extend my gratitude to all my teachers and professors who shaped me into who I am today, and to **Bridget Pupillo**, whose feedback on my draft was invaluable. My colleagues, too, played an important role in helping me strengthen this work.

I am grateful to the **Atlanta Writers Club** and to the broader writing community whose camaraderie has sustained me and sharpened my craft. I am equally thankful to **Georgia Writers, the Colorful Crow Writers Community, the Cartersville Area Writers, the International Nepali Literary Society, and many others** I may have overlooked but who have been part of this journey. The **Nexus Institute of Research and Innovation (NIRI)** has also inspired me to continue writing with purpose.

My deepest thanks to all who read and offered words of endorsement, and to **Amber Lanier Nagle** for the beautiful cover design. I am grateful for the friendship of **Mandy Lewis Cantrell**, who connected me with my publisher. Finally, to **Vickie McEntire of Colorful Crow Publishing**, thank you for shepherding this book with care, vision, and faith. Working with you has been the best experience an author could hope for.

This memoir is not only mine, but also the reflection of every person who has touched my life along the way. I am humbled and grateful.

—Tulasi Acharya

About the Author

Tulasi Acharya, PhD, originally from Nepal, began his American journey in 2008. He holds a Master's in Professional Writing from Kennesaw State University, a Master's in Women's Studies, and a PhD in Public Administration from Florida Atlantic University. He also earned an MFA in Creative Writing from Georgia College. Dr. Acharya currently teaches English at South Georgia State College.

An accomplished multilingual author, Dr. Acharya has published over a dozen books across multiple genres. His debut English novel, *Running from the Dreamland*, received critical acclaim, and his bestselling Nepali novels, *Mochan* and *Swapnabhumi*, reflect his literary versatility in both Nepali and English. His academic and creative work has been published by leading publishers, including Routledge and Lexington Books, an imprint of Bloomsbury Academic.

Dr. Acharya's short stories have earned honors such as the Certificate of Excellence from the University of New Hampshire and have appeared in numerous literary journals and newspapers, including *The Kathmandu Post*, *The Himalayan Times*, *The Rising Nepal*, and the *MSU Roadrunner Review*. In recognition of his literary achievements in the global Nepali community, he received the **INLS (International Nepali Literary Society) Homanath Subedi Diaspora Best Literary Award**.

His writing is driven by an unwavering passion for storytelling, cultural connection, and the written word.

You can learn more about his work at:

Website: www.tulasiacharya.com
Twitter: @tulsirames
Facebook: facebook.com/apersonwithbhav

www.ingramcontent.com/pod-product-compliance
Lightning Source LLC
Chambersburg PA
CBHW051617010526
44107CB00043B/1496/J